William H. Angoff

Scales, Norms, and Equivalent Scores

EDUCATIONAL TESTING SERVICE® • PRINCETON, NEW JERSEY

Preface

This book originally appeared as Chapter 15 in the second edition of *Educational Measurement,* edited by R. L. Thorndike and published by the American Council on Education in 1971. When, in the spring of 1983, I learned that the volume was out of print and would not be reprinted, I requested and was generously granted permission by ACE to submit the chapter elsewhere. Educational Testing Service expressed willingness to serve as the publisher. Hence this book.

Republication of the chapter, "Scales, Norms, and Equivalent Scores," will, we hope, provide a continuing reference for those students of psychometrics who are interested in and occupied with the very important area of test standardization and its subareas of scale definition, score interpretation, and equating. The original intent was to offer an integrated description of the state of the art by covering the various, sometimes fugitive viewpoints, methods, and techniques of test standardization. Thus, the chapter was meant to serve as a handy reference to ideas scattered through an extensive psychometric literature. As it turned out, it also served as a useful guide to the theory and methods of score equating, a subject of burgeoning interest in the 1970s. Along with other chapters of the Thorndike book, it also probably served to punctuate the end of an era in which classical test theory was giving way to the newer item response theory as a way of thinking about and operating with test scores.

This publication gives me the opportunity to express my deep appreciation to those who were so patient and helpful in reviewing the chapter and making invaluable suggestions for revision when it was first written: E. Elizabeth Stewart, Richard W. Watkins, John A. Keats, Jerome E. Doppelt, and, especially, Robert L. Thorndike.

William H. Angoff

February 1984

Contents

Introduction

One of the principal difficulties encountered in the interpretation of test scores is that the varieties of scales on which they are expressed and the varieties of groups on which the scales are defined are almost as numerous as the tests themselves. The result is that it is virtually impossible for the test user to develop a practical familiarity with all the scales that he would have occasion to use. By way of contrast, the problems of interpretation of physical measurements that the typical man in the street uses every day—height, weight, temperature, and time, for example—are quite different and considerably simpler. For him, the number of types of scales that he encounters and uses frequently is much more limited. He therefore has the opportunity to develop a skill and ease with the units of his scales and does not need to make frequent reference to manuals that describe their characteristics. He has no need to familiarize himself with the definitions and descriptions of the scales, nor does he need to familiarize himself with details about the precision of the scales. A glance at the measuring instrument itself or, at most, a trial application of the measuring instrument is sufficient to give him the information he needs. Similarly, he has little need for "tables of norms" or for detailed descriptions of the appropriate uses of his "tests." His direct and frequent experience with them provides sufficient guidance for him in the large majority of instances.

The problems of measurement in psychology and education, however, are quite different. Unlike the user of the common physical measurements, the test user does require detailed information and guidance if he is to avoid the kinds of errors that are typically made in using test scores. In part, the need for detailed information is attributable to the very nature of educational and psychological measurement. In part, also, it arises from the multiplicity of characteristics for which measurement is sought and from the multiplicity of tests that are designed and available to measure these characteristics. The test user must recognize that measurement in education is extremely imprecise in comparison with the more common types of physical measurement and that the various kinds of instruments used in education differ markedly in precision; he also must know how to evaluate this precision. He needs to know what kinds of uses of tests are appropriate for his purpose, what kinds are inappropriate, and how to get maximum information from his measurements. To do this he needs to understand the meaning of the score itself and what it represents, how it relates to other measurements of the same dimension made for the same individual at other points in time, how it relates to the measurement of the same dimension for other individuals, how it relates to and how it can be used with measurements of different dimensions, and what the nature of the evaluative information is that he himself needs to guide his decisions. All of this, and more, is needed to give the score the meaning it must have in order to be useful. And, clearly, meaning is essential, for without meaning the score itself is useless; and, without a meaningful score to transmit the value of the test performance, the test ceases to be a measuring instrument and becomes merely a practice exercise for the student on a collection of items.

This work is devoted to a discussion of some of the devices that aid in giving test scores the kind of meaning they need in order to be useful as instruments of measurement. For the purpose of this discussion it may be helpful to consider a complex testing program or a system of test offerings, part or all of which are administered at various times to heterogeneous groups of examinees. A first requirement for the transmission of the scores is that an appropriate scale structure be defined. This process of definition will be denoted by the term *scaling*. Also, since test scores, even when appropriately scaled, have limited meaning and since it will be necessary for the test users to interpret these scores in order to use them for assessment and possible later action, a second requirement is that special *norms* or other interpretive guides be prepared that will give meaning to the scores, sometimes as an inherent characteristic of the scale. Finally, since it may be necessary to have available several forms of each of the tests, a third requirement is that provision be made for the maintenance and perpetuation of the scale on which scores on the first form are reported, even as new forms are introduced and old ones withdrawn from active use. The operation involved in maintaining the scale is carried out by *equating* or *calibrating* each new form to one or more of the existing forms for which conversions to the reference scale (i.e., the reporting scale) are already available. Since all three concepts—scaling, norming, and equating—are separable, in this discussion the matter of *norms* is treated separately from that of *scales,* and the latter in turn is treated separately from the matter of *equating* and *calibration.* The problems of *comparable scores* are given separate treatment but within the context of the equating of nonparallel tests.

1. Scaling

Unlike the more common physical dimensions, for which well-established and generally satisfactory scales exist, the educational and psychological attributes for which it is wished to produce scales bring with them special problems that are not only complex but apparently unyielding as well. The concepts underlying some of the physical scales—those, for example, that are used to measure length and weight—have a direct counterpart in one's daily experience and seem to offer relatively obvious definition. The notion that one bar of steel is twice as long as a second bar is a meaningful one, easy to transmit and understand, even without the definition or the original derivation of the system of units for measuring them. The fact that this notion is implied when one says that the first bar measures six feet and the second only three derives from a willingness to accept the concept of zero length and a willingness to agree on an operation that defines the distance denoted as one inch, for example, at one part of the yardstick as equal to the distance denoted as one inch at any other part of the yardstick.

Mental measurement enjoys no such advantages. The zero point is by no means as obvious here as it is in physical measurement. Indeed it is difficult to imagine what might be meant by the absence of a mental ability, and one may even question whether the very concept of "amount" of mental ability has any meaning. In any case, a zero raw score on a mental test would certainly not signify "zero ability," since the raw score is necessarily a function of those items that appear in the test. Similarly, there is no assurance that equal differences between scores in different regions on the scale of a psychological test represent equal differences in units of ability. Suppose, for example (to adapt from an illustration suggested informally by F. M. Lord), Mary can type 20 words a minute; Margaret can type 30 words a minute; Jean, 50; and Julia, 60. Margaret's score exceeds Mary's by 10 units and Julia's score exceeds Jean's by 10 units. In the obvious sense, perhaps, the units are equal, and, therefore, it can be concluded that Julia's typing ability exceeds Jean's by the same amount that Margaret's typing ability exceeds Mary's. However, there may be other ways to define the units of typing ability besides the direct count of the number of words typed per unit of time. Suppose Mary can increase her typing speed from 20 to 30 words a minute after a week's practice while it takes Jean four weeks of practice to increase her speed from 50 to 60. In this sense, the difference between Mary's and Margaret's abilities is only one-fourth the size of the difference between Jean's and Julia's abilities. Then again, suppose 99 percent of those who have completed a semester's course in typing can do 20 words a minute or better and 97 percent can do 30 words or better; while only 40 percent can do 50 words and only 20 percent, 60. Perhaps, then, the difference (40 minus 20) between Jean and Julia should be taken to be 10 times greater than the difference (99 minus 97) between Mary and Margaret or, perhaps, taken to be some indirect function of the differences in percentages that have just been observed.

The fact that the scales used in psychological measurement are not known to be characterized by equal units and a real zero point (i.e., that they are not ratio scales), or by equal units alone (i.e., that they are not interval scales), has led some writers (e.g., Stevens, 1951) to maintain that the usual kinds of statistical treatments that are meaningful with ratio and interval scales are not meaningful in the case of psychological measurement. Lord (1953), on the other hand, has argued that statistical operations and the conduct of significance tests could be carried out appropriately and meaningfully even if the system of numbers were only nominal in character; that is, even if they represented identification numbers like those on the backs of football players—numbers that could not, by any stretch of the imagination, be considered to represent a scale.

Some consideration also should be given to the contention that the problem of inequality of units is not as unique to psychological measurement as it may appear. The same problem may be found in physical measurement. For example, it was just pointed out that the difference in typing speeds of 40 and 50 words a minute could be taken to be 4 times as great as the difference between 20 and 30 words a minute, if it were found that an improvement in speed from 40 to 50 takes 4 times as long as an improvement from 20 to 30. In the same sense it could be argued that in a certain context the distance from 30 to 68 inches should be taken as 15 times the distance from 18 to 30 inches, instead of about 3 times the distance, because people take about 15 times as long to achieve the former growth as the latter. The significant point here is that there is nothing "natural" in the equality of physical units; "equal" units are equal in psychological *or* in physical measurement only because there is an arbitrarily agreed on definition and convention that is both convenient and useful to us and also one that satisfies certain empirical tests that are implied by the model.

Accordingly, score scales for various psychological tests have been defined to have approximately equal units in some special sense. For example, they have been defined in terms of the performance of a particular group of individuals, either with or without a transformation of the distribution shape. However, in such instances, as Lord[1] pointed out:

> ... the claim for equality of score units can no longer be justified on an external operational basis. Such score scales can be said to have equal units of ability only if we are willing arbitrarily to define the ability in terms of the scale itself. However, such a definition of ability, while not indefensible, cannot hope to be generally accepted since the units of ability would vary with the group tested as well as with the choice of the measuring instrument.

The group for which the test is intended may easily change in the course of time and will not necessarily—indeed, it is not likely to—continue to be as appropriate a fundamental reference point as it may have appeared to be initially. If the transformation of raw to scaled scores is not linear—that is to say, if the intent is not to retain the original distribution shape—but is so designed as to yield, for example, a normal distribution for the reference group, there are additional considerations. There is some question that the assumption of a normal distribution in particular is appropriate, especially when selective processes have been active on the population, as they so often are. Also, the transformation to a normal shape, or to any other shape, can mask many of the indications of poor (or good) test construction. It is an elementary fact that no amount of stretching and compressing the score scale will improve the differentiating power of the test in a range of the scale where the test itself fails to differentiate adequately. On the other hand, this consideration, arguing as it appears to do for the retention of the raw score scale, or some linear transformation of it, also argues that the scale separations between successive raw scores are all equal. This is, of course, true, but only in the most literal and specific sense. In the more general sense, the notion of the equality of raw score units clearly violates one's sense of an underlying scale since the raw score scale separations are the result of the interaction of the particular items that happen to have been put in the test and therefore have no generality.

The arbitrary nature of psychological scales becomes clearer when one considers the nature of the scales of measurement of physical objects:

> Physical measurement scales, such as that for weight, possess unambiguous equality of units because such equality has been operationally clearly defined for them: two weights are said to be equal if they balance when placed on a suitable weighing device; one weight is said to be twice another if one of the former will balance two of the latter. [Typing ability] can be

[1] Informal communication, October 1950.

measured on a scale that has the same properties as the scale of weights, if we are willing to accept the requisite operational definition of this ability [for example, the number of words correctly typed per minute]. Problems arise in mental measurements either because (a) experts cannot agree on a clear operational definition of the ability to be measured or (b) the ability is defined in terms of operations for which the symbolic processes of addition or multiplication can be given no useful operational meaning. Any set of measurements can be expressed in terms of a scale with equal units, in some sense, if only we can agree on a definition in operational terms of what is meant by equality.[2]

Much of the work of the experimentalists in psychology during the latter nineteenth and early twentieth centuries was directed at the problem of defining equal psychological units and studying the relationship between those units and the corresponding units of physical measurement. Much of Thurstone's work in the scaling of judgments and attitudes also was concerned with testing the notion that psychological scales, if properly derived, might achieve some of the characteristics of the more advanced physical scales. His work on the law of comparative judgment (Thurstone, 1927) and his work on the method of equal-appearing intervals (Thurstone, 1928b; Thurstone & Chave, 1929) are attempts to develop such scales. The applications of his method of absolute scaling (Thurstone, 1925) led him to estimate the zero point of intelligence (Thurstone, 1928a) in the hope that the essential characteristic of the ratio scale could be found to apply to psychological measurement. Later developments in the concepts of scaling include the work of Guttman (1950) whose studies of attitude statements led him to define a scale as a system of units in which knowledge of the score would reproduce, within a limited margin of error, the actual responses to the attitude statements. As has been pointed out above, a variety of score scales have been proposed for use with psychological tests. Some of these are defined to have approximately equal units in some particular sense. Others lay claim to value because they possess special qualities—meaning in terms of the performance of defined and well-known groups of people or meaning in terms of the judged quality of the performance tested. Still others have been proposed which lay claim to value because they are "unencumbered" by meaning. The most commonly known scales of these various types are described below.

Raw Score Scale

In the operational sense the number of items answered correctly, with or without a correction for guessing, may be considered a scale in its

[2]*Ibid.*

own right; that is, it may be asserted that one point of score will be considered to represent the same amount of ability wherever it occurs on the score scale. Therefore, a score difference of a given number of points is by definition the same at whatever score level it occurs. This is clearly an arbitrary definition, but then all other definitions are similarly arbitrary. Nevertheless, it is important to recognize that raw scores as such have little if any generality, since they are a product of the items contained in the test. On the one hand, this characteristic of the raw score scale is considered by some to be useful, because the flaws in the test—e.g., its inappropriate difficulty for the groups for which it is intended—will be immediately apparent and will serve to motivate the press for a more appropriate test. On the other hand, it is considered by others to be a disadvantage for the very reason that it has no generality. Moreover, unless there is and will continue to be only one form of the test, the use of raw score scales can prove to be a source of confusion to the test user. Because of the natural and expected variation in difficulty from form to form, a raw score of given value will not always have the same meaning or represent the same level of ability. The form of the test would have to be specified and its characteristics known and kept in mind by the test user. The need to keep track of this additional information can prove to be cumbersome. The solution here is to adopt a reliable system of equating test forms that will make it possible to translate all forms into a common score scale. But since, in this case, all but one of the forms would require some adjustment of the raw scores, it would seem less confusing to convert raw scores on *all* forms to an arbitrary scale that is different from any of the raw score scales.

The raw score scale is perhaps the most obvious example of a scale that has no inherent meaning and cannot be interpreted without some kind of supporting data. Such data may be normative in the sense that they describe the performance of groups of individuals whose characteristics are known to the test user, or they may be functional in the sense that they indicate minimum score levels that are considered acceptable for entering or completing some activity or for receiving special recognition. Ideally, of course, both kinds of data should be made available whenever applicable.

Percentage-Mastery Scale

The scores reported on this scale are taken to represent an absolute kind of judgment that the student has mastered some percentage of the subject matter under consideration. Thus if, for example, the student earned a percentage grade of 85, it is said that his examination paper gives evidence that he has mastered 85 percent of the material covered by the examination. If he earns a grade of 63, then this is taken to mean that he has mastered 63 percent of the material. And so on. In addition, it is sometimes the custom to specify some percentage as one that would represent a minimum degree of mastery to be called "passing" and perhaps another one to be called "honors." Although this type of percentage scale is still widely used in schools and colleges, there is general agreement among test specialists that it is one of the poorest ways in which to express test performance. One of the principal objections to it is that the "absolute" character of the scale is illusory. Since it is impossible to set finite limits on knowledge, it is logically false to think that a student has mastered some percentage of that knowledge. On the other hand, if, for the purpose of the test, certain defined limits of knowledge are agreed upon, then it is possible that the percentage-mastery scale may be useful. However, careful thought would have to be given to the appropriateness of the scale of numbers to the particular universe of knowledge sampled by the test, and the percentage-mastery figures for different levels of acceptability would have to be worked out, keeping in mind the particular purpose of the test and the nature and quality of the group. Certainly what is known about the variety of the types of uses and the variety of standards for a test that is widely used would argue that one set of standards of acceptability for all purposes may not be realistic. Therefore, either the percentage-mastery scale would have to be considered appropriate only for tests with highly specific purposes, or there would have to be a different specific scale (derived from a different definition of "pass") for each purpose for which the test is to be used—a solution which is almost certain to invite confusion.

There are additional hazards in the use of a general percentage-mastery scale that could lead to misinterpretation and misuse if they are not anticipated. For example, the use of a common set of percentages for more than one test fails to take into consideration the relative difficulty of the group of items comprised by the test. There will naturally be variation in difficulty from test to test, and what appears to be 85 percent competence in one test may, for example, actually represent only 69 percent competence on another more difficult test. Finally, the use of an "absolute standard" implies a unanimity among standard setters that most certainly does not exist. Again depending on the use to which the test and the mastery scale is put, it may be advisable to set the percentage values based on the results of a controlled poll of experts. In general, however, because of its extremely unrealistic and misleading character, the percentage-mastery scale would best be avoided entirely in choosing a system for transmitting and reporting scores.

It is interesting to note that the percentage-mastery scale is one of the few scales used in educational measurement that makes reference to a norm in the sense of a standard or goal of achievement. Most of the educational test scales are defined in terms of a statistical norm, that is to say, in terms of the performance of a defined "norms group." Some scales, like the percentile-derived linear scale described below, are dependent *both* on goals and standards of performance as well as on statistical data. This simultaneous use of two apparently unrelated types of reference points for defining scales of measurement is not unique. The conventional mode of expressing visual acuity, for example, makes use of letters of such size and shape that they can be read without error by the average person with clinically normal eyesight (after correction to his optimum level of acuity). In this example, the "average person" represents the statistical norm, a referent in terms of *performance as it exists;* the notion, "clinically normal eyesight," represents the desired standard of performance, a referent in terms of *performance as it should be.*

Linear Transformation (Standard Scores)

The unadjusted linear transformation, apparently first used by Hull (1922), is one of the simplest of all the formal scaling methods. The test is administered to a group of individuals who are considered in some sense to be a standard reference group. Sometimes they are drawn at random from a defined population with certain specified characteristics; sometimes they represent a readily and conveniently available group of individuals who are considered to be similar in most important respects to the population for which the test is intended.

Once the scale-defining, or standardization, group has been agreed on and the choice of the system of units has been made, the method of scaling is a simple one involving only a relocation of the raw score mean at the desired scaled score value and a uniform change in the size of the units to yield the desired scaled score standard deviation. Since the transformation to scaled scores represents a change only in the first two moments of the distribution, it exerts no effect on the shape of the raw score distribution. If the raw score distribution is normal, then it remains so after conversion. Similarly, if it is skewed either positively or negatively, or if it is platykurtic, leptokurtic, multimodal, etc., it remains so even after conversion. The method does not seek to transform the units of the raw score scale to some other system in which the units are taken in some sense to be equal. In the linear transformation the separation between successive raw score units, or between scaled score units corresponding to successive raw scores, is considered equal only in the operational sense that each score represents one more item answered correctly than the preceding score.

Once the scale-defining group has been tested, its raw score mean and standard deviation are entered into the fundamental linear scaling equation which states that the standard-score deviate for any given scaled score equals the standard-score deviate for its corresponding raw score for the group (ω) chosen as the standardization group. Thus, $z_{c_\omega} = z_{x_\omega}$, or

$$\frac{C - M_{c_\omega}}{s_{c_\omega}} = \frac{X - M_{x_\omega}}{s_{x_\omega}}.$$

Then $C = AX + B$, converting raw scores on Form X to the scale (C), in which $A = s_{c_\omega}/s_{x_\omega}$ and $B = M_{c_\omega} - AM_{x_\omega}$. The values of M_{c_ω} and s_{c_ω} are arbitrarily chosen and assigned. The conversion equation is the equation of a straight line in which A represents its slope and B its intercept—i.e., the point on the ordinate at $X = 0$ where it is intersected by the line.

A few of the tests for which scores are reported on a linear derived scale with mean and standard deviation preassigned and defined in terms of a basic standardization group are: the Scholastic Aptitude Test and the Achievement Tests of the College Board ($M_{c_\omega} = 500$, $s_{c_\omega} = 100$), the Army General Classification Test ($M_{c_\omega} = 100$, $s_{c_\omega} = 20$), and the Cooperative Achievement Tests that were developed in the 1960s ($M_{c_\omega} = 150$, $s_{c_\omega} = 10$).

Percentile-Derived Linear Scale

Occasionally it is desired to report scores on a scale in which specified scores have preassigned normative meaning—normative in the sense of performance as it exists *as well as* normative in the sense of what is set as a standard. For example, it may be decided that the minimum passing score on a qualifying test be fixed at 70—a number that is often taken by the public to represent minimum acceptable performance—*and* that some percentage, say 65 percent, will pass. It also may be decided that the scaled score 95 will represent honors performance and that only 10 percent will receive honors grades. In order to produce a scale that will represent these characteristics, a distribution is formed of the raw scores on the test and the 65th and 90th percentiles are determined. Say that the test consists of 150 items and that the 65th and 90th percentiles are found to be 89 and 129 respectively. Two equations are written representing the transformation of the raw scores to the scale, again following the linear form $C = AX + B$: $95 = A(129) + B$ and $70 = A(89) + B$. Solving the equations for A and B, it is found that $A = .625$ and $B = 14.375$. By definition, the scale of scores resulting from this transformation will assign passing scores of 70 and above to the upper 35 percent of the group tested and honors scores of 95 and above to the upper 10 percent of the group tested. It should be understood, however, that the scale satisfies only those points that were fixed and no others. For example, a raw score of zero, it is noted, earns the examinee a scaled score of 14; a perfect raw score earns the examinee a scaled score of 108. If it is desired to fix these values also—for example, if it is desired that a raw score of zero convert to a scaled score of zero and that the maximum raw score of 150 convert to a scaled score no higher than, say, 99 or 100[3]—then to impose these additional restrictions will mean that the conversion will no longer be linear throughout. (A linear conversion results from the imposition of no more than two constraints.) There will be one conversion equation operating between scaled scores of zero and 70, another, as already calculated, operating between 70 and 95, and a third between 95 and the agreed-upon scaled score maximum.

In the procedure just described the values of 70 and 95 were—or could have been—defined in the sense of a standard, as scores that should, in some sense, be reached by no more, or no less, than certain fixed percentages of individuals. The determination of the raw scores *attaching* to those percentages, however, was normative in the sense of performance as it exists, since it was made from data resulting from the actual administration of the test. But the scale need not have been dependent on such data at all. It could have been decided on the basis of a careful review and scrutiny of the items themselves, leading to the judgment that the lowest acceptable, or passing, raw score should be set at some agreed-upon value and that the lowest raw score to be designated honors should be set at some other agreed-upon value. These two raw score values corresponding to the desired scaled score values then would be used to form the simultaneous equations, $C_1 = AX_1 + B$ and $C_2 = AX_2 + B$, and solved to determine the values of A and B of the line transforming raw scores to scaled scores.

A systematic procedure, due to L. R Tucker,[4] for deciding on the minimum raw scores for passing and honors might be developed as follows: keeping the hypothetical "minimally acceptable person" in mind, one could go through the test item by item and decide whether such a person could answer correctly each item under consideration. If a score of one is given for each item answered correctly by the hypothetical person and a score of zero is given for each item answered incorrectly

<hr>

[3]The value of 100 is sometimes avoided because of the connotation it carries of perfect performance, which could be confused with perfect knowledge.

[4]Personal communication, c. 1952.

by that person, the sum of the item scores will equal the raw score earned by the "minimally acceptable person." A similar procedure could be followed for the hypothetical "lowest honors person."[5]

With a number of judges independently making these judgments it would be possible to decide by consensus on the nature of the scaled score conversion without actually administering the test. If desired, the results of this consensus could later be compared with the number and percentage of examinees who actually earned passing and honors grades.

Percentile Rank Scale

Very likely the most familiar scale for reporting test scores is the percentile rank scale, which gives the percentage of individuals in a particular group scoring below the midpoint of each score or score interval. The precise percentile rank is obtained by totaling the frequencies for all the scores below the particular score plus half the frequencies at the score and dividing by the total number of cases. Sometimes the group on which the percentile ranks are based is assumed to be a random sample of a more general population; sometimes it is a more specialized group chosen for its possession of characteristics similar to those of the individuals to be evaluated. Percentile ranks are essentially self-interpreting and are used for making relative (i.e., normative) types of evaluations of the individual's performance. Distributions of percentile ranks for the groups on which the ranks are based are necessarily rectangular. The percentile rank scale itself is clearly ordinal and, according to most points of view, its units are unequal since they are intended to provide equal proportions of a group, not equal intervals on a scale of ability.

Normalized Scale
(Normalized Standard Scores)

It was pointed out earlier that since the properties of the raw score scale, or a linear transformation of the raw score scale, are dependent on the characteristics (e.g., difficulties and intercorrelations) of the particular items that happen to have been chosen for the test, it is frequently considered to be advantageous to transform the scale to some other

[5]A slight variation of this procedure is to ask each judge to state the *probability* that the "minimally acceptable person" would answer each item correctly. In effect, the judges would think of a number of minimally acceptable persons, instead of only one such person, and would estimate the proportion of minimally acceptable persons who would answer each item correctly. The sum of these probabilities, or proportions, would then represent the minimally acceptable score. A parallel procedure, of course, would be followed for the lowest honors score.

system of units that would be independent of the characteristics of the particular test and, in the sense of a particular operational definition, equally spaced. The assumption underlying the search for equal units was that mental ability is fundamentally normally distributed and that equal segments on the base line of a normal curve would pace off equal units of mental ability. McCall (1939) seems to be the one who is principally associated with this kind of scale, although others, including Flanagan (1939, 1951), Kelley (1947, pp. 277–284), Pearson (1906), E. L. Thorndike (Thorndike, Bregman, Cob, & Woodyard, 1927, pp. 270–293), and Thurstone (1925), also have argued for it or used it in their research. Operating on the assumption that the normal curve is characteristic of homogeneous groups that have not undergone prior selection, McCall proposed that a group of 12-year-olds be chosen at random from the population and defined as the standard group. The members of this group are tested, a distribution is formed of their scores, and mid-percentile ranks are attached to their scores, which are then transformed to normal deviate scores corresponding to those percentile ranks but with a preassigned mean of 50 and standard deviation of 10. The resulting scale is the well known *T-scale*. The numbers 50 and 10 are arbitrarily assigned, of course; any other reasonable pair of numbers, such as 500 and 100, 100 and 20, 25 and 5, etc., would do as well. In general, however the standardization group is defined and whatever the sytem of numbers for the scale may be, the method is essentially as just described and the result essentially the same; that is, a normalized score corresponding to any given raw score is the normal deviate (or a linear transformation of the normal deviate) that has the same percentile rank as does the given raw score.

The procedure for normalizing a frequency distribution is generally as follows: mid-percentile ranks, or relative cumulative frequencies (i.e., percentages of cases falling below the lower limits of successive score intervals) if that is more convenient, are computed (as in table 1) and plotted and smoothed. If the distribution is plotted on arithmetic graph paper (ordinary graph paper), the points will fall in an S-shaped pattern. It is preferable, therefore, to plot the points (as in figure 1) on normal probability paper, which tends to rectify all bell-shaped distributions (it is designed to yield a straight line for all distributions that are strictly normal) and thereby to simplify the smoothing. Smoothing is usually done by hand with the aid of an appropriate French curve or spline. There are very few guidelines available to achieve the desired results of smoothing except to say that the smoothed curve should in general sweep through the points in such a way as to equalize the divergences of the points on either side of the line. (Ideally, the smoothed distribution

11

should preserve all the moments of the observed distribution.) Beyond this general rule the judgment of the person working with the data will determine the degree to which irregularities in the data are defined as such and smoothed out.

Distributions may also be smoothed analytically before they are plotted. Analytical methods may be preferred to hand smoothing because they *are* analytical and do not depend on the subjective judgment of the test specialist. One such method, developed by Cureton and Tukey (1951), which preserves parabolic and cubic trends within successive sets of points, involves a rolling weighted average of frequencies. In order to determine a new smoothed frequency, f_i', in interval i, the method involves multiplying the weights, $-2/21, 3/21, 6/21, 7/21, 6/21, 3/21$, and $-2/21$, respectively, by the frequencies, $f_{i-3}, f_{i-2}, f_{i-1}, f_i, f_{i+1}, f_{i+2}$, and f_{i+3}, and summing the products. A corresponding 5-point formula makes use of the weights, $-3/35, 12/35, 17/35, 12/35$, and $-3/35$, respectively, for the frequencies, $f_{i-2}, f_{i-1}, f_i, f_{i+1}, f_{i+2}$. (Tukey suggested smoothing the square roots of frequencies and then squaring the smoothed values.) Another method, which is at present appropriate only to rights-scored tests, is derived from the negative hypergeometric distribution (Keats, 1951; Keats & Lord, 1962). Keats has pointed out that "whereas all other methods will tend not to give more stable estimates of percentiles, this method, when appropriate, will reduce the standard error of the estimates obtained below that for either smoothed or unsmoothed distributions."[6]

Difficulties in smoothing, and therefore with the normalizing procedures in general, are frequently encountered near the ends of the distribution where data are relatively scant; and thus percentile rank values, and consequently normalized scores, must be estimated, tempering meager data with judgment or, in extreme instances, extrapolating without the benefit of any supporting data.

Once the smoothed ogive is available, new percentile-rank values are read from the curve at the midpoint of each score interval and recorded. Finally, normal deviate values (z_n) corresponding to the new percentile ranks are read from the table of the normal curve and transformed to the scale (C_n) having the desired mean, M_c, and standard deviation, s_c, by the formula, $C_n = s_c z_n + M_c$. The procedure is illustrated in table 1 and figure 1.

The transformation to a normal distribution is *not* considered advantageous when there is reason to believe that the peculiarities in the shape of the raw score distribution reflect actual peculiarities in the distribution of ability of the group tested. For example, if the group is a

[6]Personal communication, November 1967.

TABLE 1

Normalization of Scores on Form 4a of the STEP Mathematics Test

Raw Score	Frequency	Cumulative Frequency	Percent Below	Percentile Rank (Figure 1)	Normal Deviate	Scaled Score $M = 50; s = 10$
50	1	680	99.9	99.82	2.91	79
49	5	679	99.1	99.5	2.58	76
48	6	674	98.2	98.8	2.26	73
47	6	668	97.4	97.8	2.01	70
46	12	662	95.6	96.4	1.80	68
45	17	650	93.1	94.6	1.61	66
44	11	633	91.5	92.5	1.44	64
43	17	622	89.0	90.0	1.28	63
42	24	605	85.4	87.2	1.14	61
41	26	581	81.6	84.1	1.00	60
40	23	555	78.2	80.9	.87	59
39	20	532	75.3	77.8	.77	58
38	30	512	70.9	73.9	.64	56
37	22	482	67.6	70.0	.52	55
36	28	460	63.5	66.0	.41	54
35	23	432	60.1	62.0	.31	53
34	28	409	56.0	58.0	.20	52
33	25	381	52.4	54.1	.10	51
32	26	356	48.5	50.1	.00	50
31	25	330	44.9	46.1	−.10	49
30	30	305	40.4	43.0	−.18	48
29	20	275	37.5	39.8	−.26	47
28	26	255	33.7	36.0	−.36	46
27	22	229	30.4	32.7	−.45	45
26	22	207	27.2	29.8	−.53	45
25	12	185	25.4	26.5	−.63	44
24	25	173	21.8	24.0	−.71	43
23	18	148	19.1	21.2	−.80	42
22	13	130	17.2	18.9	−.88	41
21	13	117	15.3	16.5	−.97	40
20	13	104	13.4	14.2	−1.07	39
19	13	91	11.5	12.2	−1.17	38
18	12	78	9.7	10.3	−1.26	37
17	9	66	8.4	8.8	−1.35	36
16	9	57	7.1	7.0	−1.48	35
15	11	48	5.4	5.7	−1.58	34
14	13	37	3.5	4.4	−1.71	33
13	7	24	2.5	3.3	−1.84	32
12	4	17	1.9	2.4	−1.98	30
11	3	13	1.5	1.7	−2.12	29
10	5	10	0.7	1.2	−2.26	27
9	1	5	0.6	0.8	−2.41	26
8	2	4	0.3	0.5	−2.58	24
7	1	2	0.1	0.28	−2.75	22
6	0	1	0.1	0.15	−2.97	20
5	0	1	0.1	0.08	−3.16	18
4	0	1	0.1	0.04	−3.35	16
3	1	1				
2						
1						

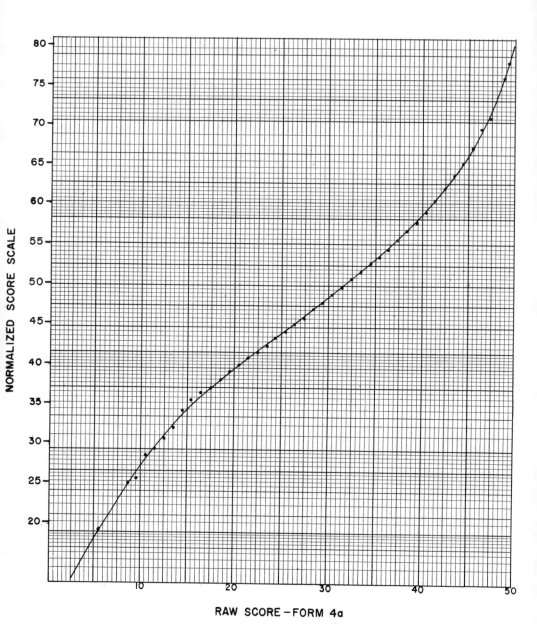

FIG. 1. Ogive for Form 4a of the STEP Mathematics Test

heterogeneous one, composed of separate subgroups of different levels and dispersions, the distribution will very likely be platykurtic even though the subgroups may individually be normally distributed. Also, if the group has been subjected to prior selection, the group tested may appear to be skewed, even though the population from which it came may originally have been normal. Moreover, there is some reason to question the assumption that the normal distribution is necessarily preferable to other distribution shapes as a basis for the definition of equality of units. Whether the distribution of ability is "basically" normal or nonnormal will never be known of course, but from an empirical analysis carried out by Keats (1951) and another analysis by Lord (1955c) it would appear that the distributions of raw scores on tests are actually more often found to be platykurtic than normal, quite possibly because of ceiling and floor effects.

There have been some well-known normalized scales in use that bear special mention here. One was the original scale for the Profile and Advanced Tests of the Graduate Record Examinations ($M=500$, $s=100$)[7], and another is the scale for the Iowa Tests of Educational Development ($M=15$, $s=5$). Still another such scale is the *stanine scale* (Flanagan, 1948, 1951), which was first used in the Air Force Aviation Psychology Program during World War II. The *stanine scale* is a single-digit scale extending from 1 to 9 (it derives its name from "standard nine") with preassigned percentages falling in each of the nine scores. The highest- and lowest-scoring 4 percent are assigned scores of 9 and 1, respectively; the next higher and lower 7 percent are assigned scores of 8 and 2; the next 12, 7 and 3; the next 17, 6 and 4; and the remaining 20 percent are assigned the stanine value of 5. The resulting distribution has a mean of 5 and standard deviation of about 2. These values come from the table of the normal curve and, except for the end intervals 1 and 9 which are open ended, they correspond to intervals half a standard deviation in width. Because it was expressed in a single digit and did not require more than one column of an IBM card, the stanine scale was especially useful during World War II at a time when data processing equipment was still in its early stages of development and could not cope as flexibly as the later versions of electronic machines with data for an individual that could not all be expressed in the 80 columns of a single card. The stanine was then, and is now, especially useful in situations where more precise determinations are not required. Indeed, because it compresses finer distributions into a nine-point scale, it tends to discourage capitalization on small differences that are not

[7]At the present time the scaled scores for the tests of the Graduate Record Examinations are converted from raw scores by linear transformation.

meaningful, in view of the possible unreliability and large error of measurement of the test.

The stanine scale has not been universally endorsed. Lindquist and Hieronymus (1964) have pointed out that for all their apparent simplicity, stanine scores are more difficult to interpret than percentile ranks, because the percentages of the distribution that fall into each stanine score category must be kept clearly in mind. Secondly, the stanine is regarded as unnecessarily coarse, particularly for reliable tests. Third, by definition, stanine distributions are equally variable from test to test and from group to group; and therefore, when, for example, they are separately derived for a test for each of a succession of grade groups as is sometimes done with stanines, they mask differences between groups with respect to variability. (It could be added that in the same sense they also mask differences in level since by definition all stanine distributions have a mean of 5.) It is pointed out that differences in rates of growth between subjects like reading, in which students have opportunities to advance on their own, and subjects like arithmetic, in which student progress is more likely to be controlled through the curriculum, are not observable when stanine scores are defined subject by subject and grade by grade. This third limitation applies, of course, to any scale that is defined separately by test and grade group. Moreover, these reservations are more properly directed at the *use* of stanines and other group-referent scales than at the scales themselves.

Another well-known system of scaled scores that is based on the area transformation is the *scaled score* system for the Cooperative Test Service, developed during the 1930s by Flanagan (1939, 1951). Operating on the premise that raw score units, or a linear transformation of raw score units, cannot in general be expected to represent equal units of ability, and on the assumption that mental ability is normally distributed in an unselected group, Flanagan proposed to transform the raw score distribution to a normal shape. This was also the position and the approach taken by McCall (1939). However, Flanagan recognized that one of the problems associated with the McCall procedure was the selection of the particular group for which the scores were to be normalized, especially where the distribution on which the scale is based contains the scores of several subgroups with different means and standard deviations. A second difficulty was that the units at the extremes of a scale based on only one distribution will tend to be unreliably scaled, since the cases on which reliable observations can be based are so scant in those regions of the scale.

It was first pointed out by Thurstone (1938) that a simple test could be made to determine whether a scale could be constructed that would simultaneously normalize the distributions of two different intact homogeneous groups. For each score the percentile rank is taken in each group and converted to its normal deviate value. If the two groups can be normalized on the same scale, then a plot of the pairs of normal deviates would fall on a straight line. This result would indicate that it might be possible to construct a scale so that other unselected homogeneous groups also would be normal on the same scale. The process of scaling the Cooperative Tests involved a procedure of adjusting the sizes of the raw score units of the tests to yield simultaneously normal distributions for each of a succession of grade levels. The Flanagan method is in principle quite similar to the method of absolute scaling, which was originally developed by Thurstone (1925) and applied to test items (rather than scores) in which the ability was assumed to be normally distributed. However, the principles of Thurstone's procedure are equally applicable to the scaling of test scores. A point of emphasis in the Flanagan scaling is that the groups for which the scale produces normal distributions must be homogeneous groups that have not been subjected to prior selection. If, for example, they were composed of two or more separate subpopulations with different means, it would not be reasonable to expect that the total combined distribution would be normally distributed. If, also, the group had undergone prior selection, it would be expected that the distribution for the remaining cases might well be skewed.

The specific procedures followed in deriving Flanagan's system of scaled scores are already described elsewhere in detail (Flanagan, 1939). Therefore, only a very brief summary of the principles and procedure of the system is attempted here. It is observed that if two overlapping normal distributions with different means and also with different standard deviations are plotted on the same scale, the (nondirectional) distance between their means (or medians) may be expressed as:

$$\frac{M_\alpha - M_\beta}{s_\alpha} = z_\alpha$$

and

$$\frac{M_\alpha - M_\beta}{s_\beta} = z_\beta,$$

where α and β refer to two groups of individuals, z_α represents the normal deviate in distribution α for the value of M_β, and z_β represents the normal deviate in distribution β for the value of M_α. From these two equations it follows that $z_\alpha s_\alpha = z_\beta s_\beta$ and $s_\alpha/s_\beta = z_\beta/z_\alpha$. That is to say, the ratio of standard deviations for α and β is the reciprocal of the ratio of their normal deviates. Therefore, in order to derive a scale that will simultaneously normalize two distributions, the percentile rank of each median is found *in the other distribution* and converted to a normal deviate, from which the relative sizes of the two standard deviations, in terms of the scaled score units, may be determined.

When a scale is sought that will simultaneously normalize *more* than two overlapping distributions, one of the groups (preferably a large, centrally located group with large variability) is chosen as the *basic* group. Then, by means of the procedure just described, a first approximation to the ratio of the scaled score standard deviations for each of the other (normalized) distributions, relative to the basic distribution, is calculated and the scale units adjusted to yield these ratios. This approximation is tested out, and the entire procedure iterated until it is judged that the newly derived values of the scaled units are in good agreement with the values just previously determined.

For the test in each subject (in the Cooperative Test series) the numerical values assigned to the scale were defined in terms of an estimate of the performance of the nation's high school students, assuming that they had attended a typical high school and had had the typical amount and kind of instruction in the subject at the usual time in their high school career. The "50-point" was the score estimated to be that of the average student so defined, but who *also:* (*a*) had an IQ between 98 and 102 on the Otis Self-Administering Test of Mental Ability, Form A (administered in grade 7); (*b*) earned a total score of 92 on the Stanford Achievement Test, Form V, at grade 8.4; and (*c*) was between 14.25 and 14.75 years old at the beginning of grade 9. The value of 10 was taken to represent the standard deviation of scores for the nation's population of students who were 14.5 years old at the beginning of grade 9, but who were otherwise unselected.

The Flanagan scaling procedure makes it clear that the process of scaling may involve two separate steps: (*a*) the determination of the interpoint distances, which Flanagan accomplished by extending the scale over a range of grade groups in such a way that each group would be normalized on that scale; and (*b*) the assignment of a set of reference numbers to the units of the scale, which he accomplished by defining the "standard group" and assigning particular values for the mean and standard deviation.

Inasmuch as the scales for all the various achievement tests of the Cooperative Test Service were constructed with the same normative meaning attaching to the means (50) and standard deviations (10), the score scales for the various tests are considered *comparable.* The *norms* for the various tests, however, are not comparable, of course, nor were they intended to be, since different types of students choose to study the various subjects represented by the tests. For example, although the score of 50 on the Intermediate Algebra Test is comparable to the score of 50 on the Trigonometry Test, since they have the same meaning in reference to the same underlying group, it would not be expected that a score of 50 would represent the same percentile rank on their respective tests for students who actually choose to study intermediate algebra and trigonometry. Since the group studying trigonometry is very likely a more highly selected and more able group than the group studying intermediate algebra, the mean scaled score for the trigonometry norms group would be higher and the percentile rank of a scale score of 50 would be lower than the corresponding values for the norms group for intermediate algebra.

Even though the scaling distributions may be restricted to students who are homogeneous in all the important respects, it is possible that in the actual situation there will be some effects—natural effects of selection, for example—operating on a distribution to cause it to skew in one direction or the other as well as to differ in mean and standard deviation. In order to allow skewness to vary, Gardner (1947) developed his system of K units, following in many respects the model of the Flanagan system but assuming the more general Pearson Type III curve instead of restricting himself, as Flanagan did, to the normal curve (which is a Pearson Type III with zero skewness).

It will be helpful to quote Gardner's (1950) own summary of the intent of his procedure: "The initial criterion under which the curves were fitted was that *the proportion of cases in each grade falling below any specific score shall remain invariant after the appropriate Type III curves have been fitted to the overlapping grade frequency distributions* [p. 42]."

By way of contrast with the foregoing curvilinear scaling methods, corresponding *linear* scaling operations retain the interpoint distances as reflected by the raw scores. In such instances the process of scaling involves merely the selection of a suitable number system to which raw scores are transformed in linear fashion. Occasionally the number system is defined in terms of the performance of a selected norms group (e.g., as was done in defining McCall's T-scale), but sometimes it is defined nonnormatively (as in the case of the College Board scale) on the basis of a conveniently available group of individuals, but not necessarily one with clear normative properties.

Age Equivalent Scale

Unlike other systems of scale unit construction which seek to transform the raw score scales to a system that will reflect equal units in some sense or to approximate a desired distribution form, age equivalent scales are intended to convey the meaning of test performance in terms of what is typical of a child at a given age, and are used principally at those ages where the function measured increases rapidly with age. The method of scaling tests to produce age equivalents generally has been carried out as follows:

1. Representative samples of children over a range of ages are administered the test to be scaled. Children falling within six months of a particular birthday are often grouped together as representing a given year group. The test should include items that are easy even for very young and dull children and extend in difficulty to items that are difficult even for much older children of advanced intelligence.

2. The mean (or median) test score of the children at each age interval is found and plotted on arithmetic graph paper against the midpoint of the age interval.

3. A smooth curve is drawn through the points in such a way as to minimize insofar as possible the distances from the points to the curve and at the same time to represent what appears to be the lawful relationship among the points. As is true of all hand smoothing operations, the accomplishment of these two objectives simultaneously will require the test specialist to exercise some compromise between them.

4. The smoothed value of each of the mean scores is assigned the age designation of the group for which it is the mean. These designations are the age equivalents; they are, in summary, the chronological ages for which the given test performances are average.

5. Finally, year-and-month values are obtained by interpolating on the curve.

Age equivalents had considerable appeal during the early history of psychological testing. Their disadvantages, however, are quite serious. There are four types of issues to consider:

In the first place, there is a basic ambiguity about age equivalents. It is an elementary fact that in any scatter diagram which represents a correlation less than unity, there are two regression lines that do not coincide. As Thurstone (1926), and later, Gulliksen (1950) pointed out, mental age may be defined in terms of either of these two lines and produce quite different results. In correlating age with test performance there is the regression of test performance on age and there is also the regression of age on test performance. Consider intelligence test scores as an example. Although the practice has been to use the former regression, mental age norms could just as logically be developed by finding the mean age of children who reach specified levels of performance and assigning those mean ages to the specified levels of performance. The mental age units corresponding to the different levels of performance would be different for the two regressions, and the interpretations attaching to these mental ages also would be different. For if the regression of performance on age is used, as it usually is, the individual who scores above the mean, for example, would be judged to be more outstanding than if the regression of age on performance were used. Depending on which regression one used, the mental age interpretation given to the *same test score* would be different. Moreover, the lower the correlation between age and test performance (as a consequence, for example, of the unreliability of the test), the greater will be the discrepancy between the two types of interpretation.

Second, the use of the age curve fails to take into account the variation about that curve. If the correlation between age and test is high and the variation about the regression line small, then a child who stands at, say, the 95th percentile in his age group may appear, for example, to be two years advanced beyond his age. If, on the other hand, the correlation between age and test score is low and the variation about the regression line large, then the same child who stands at the 95th percentile in his age group will appear to be *more* than two years advanced beyond his age. If one computes an IQ as ratio of mental to chronological age he will, as a result, earn a higher IQ. In general, when the correlation between age and test score is low, children are perceived to be more extreme—more advanced *or* retarded—than when the correlation is high. The difficulty is that the age equivalent can give a distorted and exaggerated impression of a child's level of advancement or retardation, the more so if the test is unreliable, or for other reasons relatively uncorrelated with age. Moreover, although the age equivalent is purportedly a normative measure of an individual's performance, it fails to tell one, as percentile-rank-within-age tables would, how rare his performance is.

There is still a third problem in the interpretation of age equivalents, such as mental ages. An age equivalent is meaningful only if there exists an age for which the given test performance, denoted by the age equivalent, is average. To say that an intelligence test performance of a six-year-old child represents a mental age of nine may seem reasonable, because the average nine-year-old does indeed perform at that level on the test. But what shall be used as the age equivalent for a comparably superior sixteen-year-old? Since performance on intelligence tests flattens out during adolescence and shows little further gain associated with age, there probably exists *no age* at which the average performance equals his. This limitation in age equivalents is made clear by Terman and Merrill (1937, p. 30) and also by Thurstone (1926).

Finally, it should be pointed out that the very notion of a "mental age" that conveys the meaning of the same intellectual performance irrespective of chronological age is at variance with what is known about the psychology of the individual. While it is true, for example, that some six-year-old children can perform as well as the average nine-year-olds on tests of general intelligence, a six-year-old child is nevertheless not like a nine-year-old, nor does he have the mental equipment of a nine-year-old, regardless of his score. Indeed, all that can be said about the bright six-year-old is that he is a bright six-year-old or, in statistical terms, that he stands, say, above the 99th percentile in comparison with other children of his age. A (normative) statement of this sort is more appropriate, since it involves a comparison within the child's own age group rather than an expression of performance in terms of what is typical of other age groups.

Grade Equivalent Scale

Another scale, similar in many of the important respects to the mental age scale, is the scale of grade equivalents. Grade equivalents are derived very much like age equivalents. First, representative samples of children in each grade for which a grade equivalent is desired are given the test in question, usually an achievement test. The test is designed to include items ranging in difficulty from those that are easy for children even in the lowest grade to those that are hard for children even in the highest grade. Ordinarily, only tests containing items of appropriate difficulty are given at each grade level, and an anchor test is used to calibrate the separate tests in terms of a single reference scale (see pp. 123–127; also, Lindquist & Hieronymus, 1964). Then the mean test score for children at each grade level is found and plotted on ordinary graph paper against the numerical designation of the grade. Next, the plot is smoothed, and the smoothed value of each of the mean test scores is assigned the grade designation of the group for which it is the mean. Paralleling the development of the age equivalents, these designations are the grade equivalents, i.e., the grades for which these test performances are average. Finally, grade-and-month (or tenth-of-grade) values are obtained by interpolating on the curve.

The disadvantages of the grade equivalent parallel those of the age equivalent. Here too, the equivocacy of the regression is a problem; depending on which regression line between grade and test performance one uses, the interpretation of the grade equivalent given to the *same test score* could be quite different. The more unreliable the test and the lower the correlation between grade and test performance, the greater will be the difference between these two interpretations. Moreover, since the grade equivalent fails to take into consideration the variation in test score about the curve relating grade and test score, the significance of the grade equivalent is not uniquely interpretable. For some tests, for example in arithmetic where the correlation between grade and test score is high, the finding that a child is two grades advanced in terms of his test performance may indicate that he stands quite high (say, at the 95th percentile) relative to his grade group. For other tests, for example in reading or in social studies where the correlations are lower, the same finding that he is two years advanced beyond his grade will indicate that he stands only moderately above his grade group. Thus, like age equivalents, grade equivalents are highly affected by the correlation between grade level and test performance, and the information that would be required to interpret an individual's relative standing in a group is simply not available in the grade equivalent as it is in the usual percentile rank distribution.

But beyond the statistics, there is a still more serious problem of interpretation from an educational point of view. To say that a sixth-grader's performance has a grade equivalent of eight is to say that he performs at the level of a student in the eighth grade. Clearly, in any subject-matter area that is closely tied to the grade level this cannot be, for the fact is that the sixth-grader has necessarily been taught *and tested* with the type of material that is appropriate to *his* grade; he has not been exposed to the kind of educational material in school that is normally given to an eighth-grader, nor has he in general had the opportunity to demonstrate his proficiency with eighth-grade material (Angoff, 1960).

There are additional problems with the grade equivalent, most of which Flanagan already has pointed out (1951):

1. It assumes that growth is uniform throughout the school year and that either no growth takes place during the summer or that growth during the summer is equal to one month of growth during the school year. There is certainly reason to doubt that these assumptions are universally justified in all subject-matter areas, or, indeed, whether they are even generally true (see Beggs & Hieronymus, 1968).

2. Grade equivalents for the low and high grades are often impossible to establish from available data and have to be obtained by extrapolation from existing observations. This is an extremely unreliable procedure and represents at best little more than educated guesses.

3. In parallel with the development of age equivalents, the grade equivalent, as mentioned above, can only be calculated where there is a grade for which the given test performance is average. Therefore, a grade equivalent for grades beyond, say, the ninth grade is meaningless for those subject-matter areas that are not taught in school beyond the ninth grade.

4. Because of the differences in correlation between age and performance from one subject-matter area to another and because of differences in the extent to which the teaching practices in the different areas are geared to particular grade levels, it is easy to come to the erroneous, indeed meaningless, conclusion that exceptional talent in arithmetic, for example, is less common than exceptional talent in reading or that growth in arithmetic is more rapid than growth in reading. As Flanagan (1951) pointed out, "the crux of the situation is that all of these methods are of necessity based on some characteristics of the distributions of obtained scores for the populations involved, and that none of these characteristics is in any sense 'fundamental,' but all are influenced by, or are a function of, arbitrary practices in instruction and curriculum organization [p. 711]." These are the factors that cause differences among the various subjects taught in school with respect to overlap from grade to grade. And it is these differences in overlap—the differences in the between-grade variability relative to the within-grade variability—that are reflected in the differences among the correlations between test scores in each of the various subjects and grade level and invalidate any statements regarding comparability across subject-matter areas.

5. The grade equivalent scale is necessarily dependent on, indeed an artifact of, the particular way in which the subject-matter area in question is introduced and the way in which it is emphasized in the curriculum throughout the grades. Differences from one school and community to another in this regard will have a profound effect on grade equivalents. Gulliksen (1950) pointed out too that

> the relationship between age and grade norms is affected by changes in the educational customs regarding promotion from grade to grade. In the early 1900's promotion was based primarily on achievement. The pupil who did not learn as rapidly as the average was not promoted. Such an educational system would give rise to a marked difference between age and grade norms, and also lead to a smaller dispersion of scores within each grade, accompanied by less overlap in the scores of adjacent grades. The present custom of promoting a pupil primarily on the basis of age will increase the resemblance between age and grade norms (or between age and grade equivalents), increase the dispersion of scores within a given grade, and produce a marked overlap in the scores of adjacent grades. Norms (or grade equivalents) that

were determined under the former system of promotion (primarily on the basis of achievement) cannot be compared with norms (or grade equivalents) established under the present system of promotion primarily based on age. Similarly, norms that have been established under limited educational opportunities, and when the illiteracy rate is high, cannot be expected to resemble norms established when the educational level of the population is increased, and the illiteracy rate is low [p. 291].

6. In general, the use of grade equivalents tends to exaggerate the significance of small differences, and in this way, as well as in other ways described above, to encourage the improper use of test scores. Because of the large within-grade variability it is entirely possible, for example, for a child who is only moderately above the median for his grade to appear on the grade equivalent scale to be as much as a year or even two years advanced. A comparison of the grade equivalents with percentile ranks would make this fact clear.

7. Some teachers tend to confuse the grade equivalent norm with a desired or ideal standard of performance and make the judgment that their class is doing satisfactory work if they are performing up to the "norm," without regard to other important and relevant factors such as the general level of intelligence of their children or other factors related to differences in curriculum emphasis. Although this kind of misinterpretation can occur with all kinds of normative data, it is probably most likely to be made when the interpretive data for the test call for the translation of test performance into a *single* grade equivalent value.

Contrary to the claims that sometimes are made for them, grade and educational (or mental) age equivalents do not provide a good basis for comparability among tests, nor do they represent a uniquely better metric than other scales, such as the normalized or linear scales, for measuring growth. There is indeed general agreement that they are inferior to percentile rank tables when it comes to the interpretation of an individual student's test scores or in comparing his standing on several tests. The principal claim that can be made for the grade and age equivalents is that they have a simplicity and directness of meaning in terms of the test user's everyday experience that are not shared by other scales. However, the difficulties and confusions that are attendant on the use of these equivalents would indicate that their simplicity is far more apparent than real and that the truly simple scales may well be those for which there has been no attempt to capitalize on the use of direct meaning. Moreover, while it is possible that direct meaning may be a highly desirable feature in a system of derived scores, the trouble is, as has frequently been pointed out, that users read into such scores more or different meanings than they actually possess.

The IQ Scale

Although the IQ as a ratio of mental age to chronological age is seldom, if at all, in use today, it will be valuable to examine its psychometric properties. The determination of the IQ for an individual, as the IQ was originally conceived, was accomplished by finding the mental age (i.e., the age equivalent) for his performance, dividing that number by his chronological age, and multiplying by 100. By definition, then, an individual is of average intelligence if his mental age equals his chronological age, giving him an IQ index of 100. To the extent that his performance is higher than would be expected for his age his IQ is higher than 100, and to the extent that his performance is lower than would be expected for his age his IQ is lower than 100.

The primary value of the IQ lies in the apparent simplicity with which it can be interpreted and explained and, also, in its built-in comparability from one age to the next. To the extent that the sampling has been adequate and comparable from one age to another in the construction of the mental age norms and to the extent that the growth pattern of intelligence, or rather of performance on the items comprised by the test, is reasonably similar from one child to the next, and, finally, to the extent that the regression of score on age is homoscedastic, the IQ remains fairly constant from age to age.

In reviewing the data for the 1937 revision of the Stanford-Binet, Terman and Merrill observed (1937, p. 40) that there was more than a chance fluctuation in the standard deviations of IQs from age to age. Five years later, McNemar (1942, p. 85) pointed out that this fluctuation was an inverse function of the differences in the variability of the difficulties of the items appropriate at the different ages. (It also may have been a function of the differences in item-test correlations at different age levels.) This fluctuation in variability means in effect that ratio IQs are *not* comparable from age to age, but than an IQ at one age may be equivalent in relative position to a somewhat higher or lower IQ at a different age. In other words, the fluctuation in variability undermined the assumption or claim of the constancy of the IQ An individual's IQ could shift from one age to the next, not because of any change in intelligence relative to other individuals of his age, but merely because of changes in the variability of test performance from one year to the next. In order to eliminate these types of fluctuations, the IQs that were developed for the 1960 L-M Revision are *deviation IQs,* rather than ratios as originally defined. Deviation IQs are essentially standard scores and as such they yield the kind of normative interpretation that is not available in the age and grade equivalents. In this respect and also in the respect that they avoid some of the statistical and educational-psychological confusions of the age equivalents, they represent a decided improvement over the ratio IQs.

The development of the deviation IQs is a fairly simple matter, conceptually. For each age group a random sample of individuals was selected and tested, and a conversion system developed to yield a mean of 100 and standard deviation of 16 for those individuals (Terman & Merrill, 1960). Assuming that a child's rank-order position in intelligence test scores remains constant from age to age, the method of reporting scores as deviation IQs, standardized with the same mean and standard deviation at each age, ensures that that child's IQ also will remain constant from one age to the next.

Except for minor procedural differences which may involve a normalization of the score distributions, the same general approach to the standardization of means and standard deviations has been followed in the development of IQ scales for virtually all of the intelligence tests that provide IQ equivalents, including the Wechsler Adult Intelligence Scale (WAIS), the Wechsler Intelligence Scale for Children (WISC), the Lorge-Thorndike Intelligence Tests, the Kuhlmann-Anderson Test, the Pintner General Ability Tests, the Otis Tests, and the California Test of Mental Maturity. Indeed, the Stanford-Binet is one of the tests that has relatively recently adopted the deviation IQ. The Wechsler-Bellevue Intelligence Scale used it as early as 1939. It is interesting that the tests do not all adopt the same value for the standard deviation of IQ within age. The WISC, for example, uses 15, instead of the value 16 that was adopted in the 1960 revision of the Stanford-Binet (Seashore, Wesman, & Doppelt, 1950). The implication of this difference is that—aside from differences in the standardization groups resulting from sampling errors, and possibly other factors—the Stanford-Binet and WISC IQs are not comparable. That is to say, high or low IQ values are rarer on the WISC than on the Stanford-Binet.

The EQ and AQ Scales

The ease of interpretation to which the ratio IQ *apparently* lent itself was quite likely influential in the development of similar indices, such as the educational quotient (EQ), which is the ratio of educational age (similar to mental age in conception but calculated for achievement in subject-matter areas) to chronological age and even the achievement quotient (AQ), which is the ratio of the EQ to the IQ, that is to say the ratio of the educational age to the mental age. The AQ appeared to represent an attempt to measure over- and underachievement in terms of a ratio of "actual achievement" to "potential ability." Flanagan pointed out (1951, p. 716) that the AQ has been discredited principally because:

(*a*) it is sensitive to random errors of measurement, norming, and scaling—the error in the AQ is larger than the error in a simple quotient like the IQ, for example, since it is the result of the combined errors in both the EQ *and* the IQ; (*b*) it is subject to errors resulting from the *differences* in the norms samples used in the standardization of the tests from which the age equivalents are obtained; (*c*) the different growth curves used to establish educational age and mental age causes difficulties, especially at the exteme ages where extrapolated values are used and where unselected age groups are hard to obtain; (*d*) other factors, such as the high correlation between intelligence and achievement tests and the variability in age at the particular grade levels at which the different subjects are taught, affect the practical value of the AQ adversely. Furthermore, the *expected* AQ differs for different values of the IQ. Because of regression effects, the expected AQ is less than 100 for IQ values above the group mean and over 100 for IQ values below the group mean. The amount of this effect is proportional to the size of the IQ deviations. As a result, AQ values are characterized by a systematic bias.

Normative vs. Nonnormative Derived Scales

In general, if one were to examine the various reasons for preferring systems of derived score scales for standardized tests rather than the original raw score scales, one would find that the reasons fall into about four principal categories (Angoff, 1962):

1. For the sake of convenience in handling test score data, it is frequently desirable to convert raw score data to scales with preassigned characteristics in round numbers that are easy to recall and easy to use. The stanine scale is a good example of a scale that possesses this characteristic, as is the IQ scale, the 50–10 scale and others.

2. As has already been pointed out, the raw score scale of a test is considered by some to be no more than an ordinal scale. Some doubt has been expressed that it should be used, for example, to compare changes in different regions of the scale. In an effort to make comparisons of this sort possible, raw score scales are converted to derived scales in which the unit separations between scores are in some operational sense equal. Tucker's proficiency scale, Flanagan's scaled score system, and Gardner's *K* scores are derived scales of this type.

3. Derived scales are used when more than one form of a test is available and the forms are used interchangeably. In such instances, it is desirable to equate the scores reported for the forms in order to make them independent of the difficulty characteristics of the form on which they were earned. It also is considered desirable to report scores on a

scale that is clearly different from, and therefore cannot be confused with, the raw score scale of any form. The derived scale, then, exists as a referent for all test forms on which scores are made interchangeable as a result of a process of equating. The College Board scale is one of a number of scale systems that purport to relate test forms in this way.

4. It usually is maintained that the raw score scale yields little or no immediate meaning of its own. For that reason, derived score scales are established in which normative meaning is directly incorporated. The scales described in the preceding discussion are scales of this type, those that derive their systems of units from the administration of the test to a *standardization group* (a group drawn as a representative or random sample of a defined population). In the sense that the knowledge of any derived score yields *inherent evaluative* knowledge of a test performance in comparison with the test performance of members of a known population, the scale is taken to be a *normative scale*. McCall's *T* scores represent a scale of this type, as do all the others that have been described so far.

There is little argument that a derived score scale is useful in a situation where there is a system of interrelated test forms. To refer to ability measures in terms of the unadjusted raw score scales of the forms when the forms are not precisely equivalent in difficulty would only invite confusion. Similarly, there is little argument that it is convenient to use a scale system that is based on a set of numbers that are easy to recall. It would be difficult to imagine why one would choose to assign a number like, for example, 81.27 as the mean of a distribution of derived scores rather than a round number like 50 or 100. Finally, there is little question that educational and psychological measurement would be vastly improved if its scales could be expressed in terms that everyone would agree represent equal units of ability. Such a scale, with units equally spaced throughout, would permit the direct comparison of score differences in one region of the continuum with score differences in any other region of the continuum.

With regard to the *normative* characteristic of the scale there has been some dispute. Generally speaking, it has been taken for granted that it is at least desirable, if not even necessary, that the system of numbers for a scale have inherent normative meaning; i.e., that it be defined in terms of the performance of a representative group of individuals. The argument is that, since such a scale gives the user immediate normative information, it is therefore more useful than one that is not normatively derived. This view has been expressed by many writers, including especially Flanagan (1939, 1951, 1953, 1962) and Gardner (1947, 1949, 1950, 1962, 1966). On the other hand, Tucker

(1953) has described the usefulness of a scale that is independent of the characteristics of reference groups, one in which meanings attaching to a test score depend on the test itself and the items it comprises. Lindquist (1953) has argued too that "the best type of scale is one that is divorced as much as possible from any normative meaning [p. 38]." Such a scale, he pointed out,

> has the very distinct advantage that if the norms change after the scale has been established ... then there is no need to abandon the scale on that account, or to rescale the test. Instead, all one need do in that case is to leave the reference scale as it was before, because it does not depend on normative meanings, and make whatever changes in the normative scales associated with it [that] happen to be appropriate [p. 38–39].

Angoff (1962) has made essentially the same point, that the commitment to a particular norms group in the definition of a scale is not only unnecessary but unnecessarily restrictive as well, since it imposes a particular kind of normative interpretation on the scores that may not always be appropriate. Angoff maintained, as Lindquist had, that any built-in normative meaning was likely to become obsolete with time and, consequently, to lead to the misinterpretation of test scores. Moreover, since only one meaning could be built into a score scale, this meaning could serve only one purpose of the test to the exclusion of all others. In general, he pointed out, scales of measurement are quite useful even when they have no inherent or definitional meaning. By way of illustration he showed that in spite of the fact that the original definition (i.e., the "meaning") of most of the commonly employed units of measurement (like inches, pounds, degrees Fahrenheit, etc.) is totally unknown—indeed, lost—to the large majority of the public, their usefulness is by no means impaired by this loss. What makes these units truly meaningful to the user is their *familiarity;* and what allows these units to become familiar and otherwise useful is the *constancy* of their meaning—the fact that an inch, for example, represents the same length on any ruler, and that it also represents the same length this year as last. Similarly, in the case of test scales the more permanent and useful meaning is the meaning that comes with familiarity. Here too, familiarity comes as a result of the successful maintenance of a constant scale—which, in the case of a multiple-form testing program, is achieved by rigorous form-to-form equating—and through the provision of *supplementary normative data* to aid in interpretation and in the formation of specific decisions, data which would be revised from time to time as conditions warrant.

Whatever the merits of normative versus nonnormative scales may be, there is little question that it is not *necessary* to derive a score scale normatively. For example, the scale may be defined in a nonnormative fashion as Guttman did (1950). The *Guttman scale,* unlike the methods of scaling described above, was developed in the context of attitude and opinion measurement and was intended primarily to determine whether a universe of attitude statements is unidimensional; that is, whether there is a singleness of meaning in an area of opinion or attitude. Unlike the methods of scaling previously described, which are primarily intended to assign a system of numerical values to raw test scores, Guttman's method is intended to determine whether a scale, as he defines it, exists. The assignment of numerical values is secondary.

A perfect scale in Guttman's sense is one in which an individual who agrees with a strong statement of attitude also will agree with a milder statement of that attitude; similarly, an individual who disagrees with a mild statement of attitude will disagree also with a stronger statement of that attitude. For example, if an individual indicates on a social-distance questionnaire that he is unwilling to have as a neighbor a member of nationality group X, he would similarly be expected to say that he would be unwilling for his child to marry a member of that nationality group. As mentioned earlier in the context of mental tests, a perfect scale is one in which a person who passes an item of given difficulty also will pass any other item of lesser difficulty; an individual who fails an item of given difficulty will fail also any other item of greater difficulty.

Knowledge of a person's score on a questionnaire (or a test) that forms a Guttman scale permits perfect reproduction of his actual responses. To the extent that the item responses are reproducible, the questionnaire is said to be homogeneous, unidimensional, and reliable in the sense that the items have high tetrachoric intercorrelations.

One of the difficulties of the Guttman approach lies in the fact that it is *deterministic* in the sense that the subject's response to each item is completely determined by his position on the scale. However, this characteristic of the Guttman model is not likely to be realized in practice, even approximately, because of the relatively large errors of measurement. An alternative approach is to assume that the *probability* of the subject giving a particular response is completed determined by (a) his position on a scale and (b) one or more constants associated with the item. In the case of ability tests the assumption is made that the probability of a correct response P is completely determined by: (a) the ability of a of the subject as measured on some scale; (b) the difficulty d of the item; and (c) its discriminating power v. In other words, P is determined by, or is a function of, a, d, and v *only*; i.e., $P = f(a, d, v)$.

The particular functional relationship to be used between the items and the ability continuum is a matter of assumption. Various suggestions for this relationship have been made, including polynomials (Lazarsfeld, 1950), the cumulative normal ogive (Lawley, 1943; Lord, 1952a, 1952b; Tucker, 1951, 1953), the logistic curve (Birnbaum in Lord & Novick, 1968), and a simpler form (Rasch, 1960). All of these models are special cases of the general latent structure model and carry with them the assumption that all the items in the test are measuring the same ability, but that chance factors affect the response pattern. Furthermore, in all of them, ability a is a property of the individual that is constant over all the items in an item domain, and d and v are properties of items which are independent of other items administered. A major hope of those using this approach is that item constants such as d and v will in fact prove to be relatively invariant over populations and that inferred ability a will be relatively invariant over different sets of items. That this hope may be realized is indicated in a study by Wright (1968). Conceivably, the flexibility afforded in scaling, norming, and equating by these invariances could well lead to some major innovations in mental measurement.

The probabilistic model chosen as an example to be given below was developed by Rasch and is algebraically the simplest. This model contains the assumption that all items are of equal discriminating power. With this assumption the parameter v may be omitted; i.e., $P = f(a, d)$. The Rasch assumption for the form of the functional relationship is: $P = a/(a+d)$, where a and d are zero or positive and, therefore, P takes on values from zero to one.

With this relationship assumed and with complete data for all subjects, it can be shown that, for estimation purposes, equal numbers of correctly answered questions imply equal ability a for the individuals tested. Hence, one could construct a two-way table to check the assumptions of the model. Rows in this table would correspond to items, and columns would correspond to raw scores. An entry in the table would be the proportion of people with a raw score corresponding to the column who correctly answered the item corresponding to the row. This proportion would be an estimate of P which is a function of the ability a of all individuals with that raw score and of the difficulty d of the item. By taking logarithms and manipulating the equation relating a and d, it can be shown that $\log\{P/(1-P)\} = \log a - \log d$. Thus if the two-way table of P's just described undergoes the transformation $\log\{P/(1-P)\}$, the resulting entries should fit a two-way analysis-of-variance model without interaction and with item and raw score level as the main effects. Furthermore, since the coefficients of $\log a$ and $\log d$ are unity, a plot of cell entries for any row against the means of the columns should produce a straight line with a slope of 45 degrees. Slopes that depart radically from 45 degrees indicate that the items are not equally discriminating. The test constructor who uses this model may wish to make such tests on his data as did Rasch (1960) in his empirical study of the model.

For data that fit the model, it is possible to estimate the ability level, a, associated with a raw score on a scale with an origin, which is simply to say that division of one ability level by another is a permissible numerical operation under the model. This is so because column averages of the table that are used to check the model are estimates of log a plus an arbitrary constant and hence may be written as log ka. Hence, by taking antilogs of the column averages, an estimate of ka may be obtained. The choice of k would not affect ratios of a's and hence a is estimated on a ratio scale (Stevens, 1951). The choice of k may be governed by numerical (or other) convenience.

Theory development in this area has taken a direction towards greater complexity to account for the varieties of tests found in practice. However, test constructors might well consider the advantages of preparing tests according to the more restrictive requirements that are necessary if the raw score, or some simple transformation of it, is to have an unambiguous and useful meaning.[8]

Another scale that follows the general probabilistic model is Tucker's proficiency scale, (Tucker, 1951, 1953; Lord, 1952a). In constructing this scale, the items of the test are first ranked in order of difficulty, and the rank order is examined for invariance with respect to different populations. This invariance, once verified, establishes the homogeneity of the domain of the test. Then for each item or homogeneous group of items, an item characteristic curve (a curve of percentage passing at each score level) is drawn against the raw score on the test, and different parts of the scale are expanded and contracted, so to speak, in order to normalize all item characteristic curves simultaneously. The score corresponding to an agreed-upon percentage-pass (e.g., 70 percent) on the item is taken to describe the scale difficulty of the item. The individual's score is the place on the scale corresponding to the group of items that he was able to respond to just barely satisfactorily.

The intent of the Tucker procedure is to establish a system of scale unit separations which, unlike the McCall T-scale, for example, will be independent of the performance of any particular group of examinees. The assignment of numercial values to the scale units then could be

---

[8]The preceding paragraphs on the probabilistic models of scaling have been contributed by J. A. Keats and R. F. Boldt.

made by any one of a number of ways, so long as the relative distances between units remain unchanged. This latter restriction implies a linear transformation, which could be derived in a normative fashion as described earlier in this section by testing some defined group of individuals to whom an agreed-upon scaled-score mean and standard deviation would be assigned, or by one of the nonnormative methods described below.

A nonnormative linear conversion to scaled scores also may be established by arbitrary decision or by agreement among judges as a result of detailed study, as described in connection with percentile-derived linear scales (pp. 8–10). In this method two raw scores are arrived at: *one,* for example, corresponding to the hypothetical minimally acceptable person and the other corresponding to the hypothetical lowest honors person. Corresponding to these two scores, a pair of scaled scores are arbitrarily chosen, such as 70 and 95, to represent passing and honors. Two simultaneous linear equations are then written, expressing the relationship between these particular raw and scaled scores, and solved for the slope and intercept values of the linear equation relating the raw scores to the scale.

The foregoing technique of setting minimum scores is applicable in many other situations, including those where scale definition is not under consideration. For example, in those situations where a single general ability test is administered to all the members of a heterogeneous group, say army recruits, and some guidelines need to be established at the outset for assignment to occupational specialties for which different levels of ability are required, judgments may be made of the probability that the minimally acceptable individual in each of the specialties will pass each item. The sum of the probabilities for each specialty then defines the minimally acceptable score for that specialty. Similar kinds of judgments also may be used to set minimum standards of ability for admission to officer candidate school or to other training programs. Later validity studies will help to verify the appropriateness of the initial cutting scores or to correct them if necessary.

There is, finally, a very simple and obvious type of nonnormative scale that is derived solely from the scores of the test itself and is useful when there are multiple forms of the test. The scale may be defined as the test score scale of the first form or, preferably, by means of a convenient but arbitrary translation of the test score units into scale scores without normative properties. For example, the mean chance score on the first form may be assigned a scaled score of 50 (or any other number) and the maximum score assigned a scaled score of 150 (or any other number). These two points define the general range of scaled scores for the first form and therefore the general range of scaled scores for all other forms that may directly or indirectly be equated to that form. The equation for converting the test scores to the defined scale is found by solving a pair of simultaneous equations in much the same way shown for the percentile-derived linear scale or for the scale derived from the judgment of minimum standards. For example, if the test in question has 200 items and the mean chance score is zero (that is, if the test scores are corrected for guessing), then the simultaneous equations will be: $150 = A(200) + B$ and $50 = A(0) + B$, from which it is found that $A = .500$ and $B = 50.00$. If the test scores are not corrected for guessing, then, assuming that the test consists of five-choice items only, the equations will be: $150 = A(200) + B$ and $50 = A(40) + B$ (the score of 40 representing the mean chance score for a test of five-choice items), from which it is found that $A = .625$ and $B = 25.00$. It should be understood that, just as the scale values are arbitrarily chosen, the test scores corresponding to those scale values are also arbitrarily chosen. For example, the raw scores corresponding to scaled scores 50 and 150 on this form might have been 0 and 200 or, indeed, *any* pair of usable values, no matter what the scoring formula may have been. Except for the changes in the numerical values of the units, this converted score scale has the very same properties that are characteristic of the raw score scale. Its advantage over the raw score scale lies in the fact that it *is* a converted score scale, clearly different from the raw scores and, by design and choice, not likely to be confused with the raw scores—a scale in terms of which raw scores from different forms have already been calibrated and are now expressed. Given such a converted score scale, the question, On what form of the test was this score of 43 earned? becomes unnecessary and, moreover, irrelevant.

There is much to be said for the point of view that the score scale should have a normative referent and yield automatic normative interpretation, particularly in the case of tests that have a highly specific purpose and for which the target population is clearly defined. However, where the test is intended for use in a variety of circumstances and for a variety of subgroups and it is desired to make the supplementary norms and validity data the vehicle for score interpretation, then it may be desirable to define the scale in terms of a set of numbers that are themselves as much divorced from normative interpretations as possible. In such instances, it will be sufficient that the important benchmarks for the scale be chosen to satisfy the criterion of convenience. In the case of the preceding illustration the scale centers about 100. It might just as well, of course, have centered about 50, or 500, or 5, or 25, or any other convenient number. The choice of the specific set of numbers for this method of scaling—or any other method of scaling—would depend on the particular purposes of the program, the need to avoid confusion with other test scales already in existence, and the reliabilities of the tests in the system.

The process of defining a scale has been observed here to be conceptually and also practically separable into at least two parts: (*a*) the definition or determination of the relative interpoint distances on the scale; and (*b*) the assignment of a system of numerical values to the benchmarks on the scale. Some of the methods that have been described here accomplish both of these purposes at once. These include, among others, the linear scale with preassigned mean and standard deviation, the percentile-derived linear scale, and the area transformation to the McCall *T*-scale or to stanines. In the case of the linear conversions to the scale, the assumption is implicit that the psychological distances between successive raw scores are equal, since the linear transformation does nothing to change the relative sizes of these distances; distances between scaled scores corresponding to successive raw scores are always equal in a linear transformation of raw scores. The process of transforming scores is intended only to change the number system. In the case of the area transformations—i.e., the transformation of the distribution to a normal curve or to a distribution of some other desired shape—not only does the scaling procedure change the number system, but at the same time it also redefines the unit separations (except, of course, in those instances where the raw score distribution already conforms to the desired shape). However, these two processes can be carried out separately and independently. It is possible in a *first step* to define the scale separations in accordance, for example, with the procedure followed by Tucker or with the procedure followed by Flanagan, and in a *separate step* to define the system of numbers in which the test scores are to be expressed. Since it would be desired to retain the scale separations that were determined in the first step, the transformation to scaled score numbers necessarily would have to be linear, either normative (by defining the values of the mean and standard deviations or by defining the values of two percentiles) or nonnormative (by defining the values of two "absolute" standards of performance or by otherwise defining arbitrarily the values of two benchmarks on the scale).

It may be useful to observe that additional distinctions may be made between the various types of scales that have been described here. For example, there are *distributive* and *nondistributive* scales, that is to say, scales based on the performance of groups of individuals and scales otherwise defined. Some of the distributive scales are *normative,* in the sense that they are based on samples of examinees systematically drawn from clearly defined populations. Others are *arbitrary,* in the sense that they are based on conveniently available groups of examinees for whom the test is appropriate but not on the results of a systematic sampling effort. By way of illustration, the College Board scale, based on the performance of the 10,654 examinees who took the Scholastic Aptitude Test in April 1941, is just such an *arbitrary distributive scale.* It is derived from a linear transformation of the raw score mean and standard deviation of an available and appropriate, and reasonably typical, group of examinees. These examinees represent a homogeneous group in the sense that they chose to take the Scholastic Aptitude Test for admission to one or more of the colleges requiring the test of their applicants. However, beyond that restricted definition, the group has no normative meaning and little if any normative usefulness. Normative comparisons are made, as they are required, against specific norms groups for whom data are collected to answer specific questions. *Nondistributive scales* are scales that are independent of the characteristics of any group of individuals. Examples of such scales are the linear derived scale, which depends on the definition of a set of standards for honors and passing, the Tucker proficiency scale, the Guttman scale, and the scale resulting from the linear transformation of a pair of arbitrarily chosen raw scores to a pair of arbitrarily chosen scaled scores.

The point also should be made, as it was earlier in this section, that the term *normative* itself has at least two separate meanings. In the sense in which it is used in this chapter, it has a statistical meaning; it refers to the actual performance of well-defined and understood groups of individuals who are used for reference, comparison, and evaluation of test scores. In this sense it refers to *performance as it exists.* In another sense the term normative refers to *standards* or *goals* of performance. The method of scaling that depends on the judgment of passing or honors is normative in that sense.

In general, it would appear that the long-term value of a test and the scale on which its scores are expressed will depend more on the measurement qualities built into the test (and consequently into the scale) and on the nature of the psychological domain from which the test items are sampled, than on any normative properties which might be embodied in the scale and be appropriate in the short term. To define the interpoint distances for a test scale after the fact, in terms of a defined group and distribution form but without regard for the psychometric properties of the test, cannot help but appear to be insufficient and, moreover, to depend on arbitrary and adventitious choice. Although it may be convenient at first to have normative information inherent in the scale, the obsolescent nature of normative data, resulting from changes in the composition of the population and/or from changes in the educational programs, soon reflects itself in a disagreement between the current norms and the existing scale (i.e., the old norms) and dramatizes the lack of fundamental and lasting significance in the original scale. Application of the Tucker-Rasch type of model, on the other hand, would permit the specification of test construction methods in order to satisfy certain desirable psychometric properties and would make possible a more general system of scale separations that would be invariant with respect to any norms population.

2. Norms: Interpretive Data

As was pointed out earlier, it is frequently the practice to incorporate normative meaning into the definition of a scale. In the preceding section, scales of this type (as well as scales not based on normative groups and therefore without normative meaning) were discussed, but only as they related directly to the matters of scale definition. In the present section, the issue of norms is central; matters relating to scales are introduced only as they bear on the norms issue.

By now it has become almost axiomatic that raw scores on a test yield no meaning unless they are accompanied by relevant supplementary data that will place the score in an appropriate interpretive context. These data take a number of forms. Some of them are solely descriptive of the test itself and include such matters as the number of items in the test, its timing and consequent speededness, its reliability and standard error of measurement, its statistical validity, the intercorrelations among its parts, and, if the scores are not raw scores but are reported on a derived scale, the nature of that scale. Such information makes it possible to evaluate the general usefulness of the test. Other kinds of interpretive data permit the evaluation of the level of score earned by a student. These data also take a number of forms. When they represent descriptive statistics that are compiled to permit the comparison of a particular score (or mean) with the scores (or means) earned by the members (or groups of members) of some defined population, the data are referred to as *norms*. Typically, norms take the form of a percentile rank distribution that makes it possible to determine an individual's *relative standing* within the defined population so that an interpretive statement such as the following may be made: Douglas is at the 98th percentile in verbal ability and at the 92nd percentile in mathematical ability in comparison with all high school seniors. Other kinds of norms, also descriptive of relative standing, are those that are reported in a manner intended to convey more concrete meaning, e.g., those that equate test score to age or to grade level. Norms of this type permit statements such as: Carolyn has a mental age of 11 years and 3 months on the Stanford-Binet and a grade equivalent of 6.7 on the Vocabulary Test of the Iowa Tests of Basic Skills.

In general, there are two kinds of meaning that have been attached to the term *norms*. One of these is associated with notions of acceptable, desired, or required *standards* or *clinical ideals*. Thus it may be said that Mr. Jones is 15 pounds overweight, meaning that he is 15 pounds heavier than *he should be.* The determination of what he should be may have been made previously on some independent basis, related to medical or athletic considerations, to the work that Mr. Jones does or is applying to do, or to some other consideration. The other kind of meaning of the term *norms,* which may lead to quite different interpretations of the same performance, is the *statistical* meaning and is the one in terms of which educational and psychological measurements are most often interpreted. Thus a test performance is said to be high or low in relation to a defined group of other individuals. The fact that the two kinds of "normative" interpretations can be quite different may be illustrated by noting that the same Mr. Jones who may be clinically overweight by 15 pounds may nevertheless be 10 pounds underweight when compared with other men of the same age, height, and morphological structure. Clearly, then, the comparison group is also clinically overweight, even more so than Mr. Jones. The possibility of confusion between norms as representing *achievement as it exists* and norms as representing *standards to be achieved* has already been noted. It is possible, for example, as Lindquist and Hieronymus (1964) have observed, that an elementary school may give more adequate attention to the study of arithmetic than to map-reading skills, and that the development of skill in map reading may be generally neglected in all schools, even in those schools where the students earn relatively high scores in map reading. In a school, then, whose average is below the norm in arithmetic and above the norm in map reading, the need for better instruction may, nevertheless, be greater in map reading than in arithmetic. Clearly, what constitutes satisfactory performance, or what is an acceptable standard, can only be determined subjectively by the school in terms of its own objectives and emphases and in terms of what may reasonably be expected of its students.

Statistical normative data may be said to satisfy more than one function. By presenting frequency distributions and other associated descriptive statistics for samples of well-defined and well-known populations of individuals, the publisher of the test makes it possible to develop a familiarity with the scale for the test. Normative data also make it possible to acquire an understanding of the dimensions in which major subgroups of the population differ and the degree to which the variables of the test are associated with classifications of the population. Finally, norms make it possible to assess the level of performance of an individual or a group and to use that assessment as a basis for decision and action.

Conrad (1950) and Schrader (1960) have both outlined certain generalizations that are appropriate to the construction of norms. The following are essentially restatements of their generalizations:

1. The characteristic measured by the test must permit the ordering of individuals along a transitive asymmetric continuum from low to high; i.e., the scale must be ordinal, at least.

2. The test must represent a reasonable operational definition of the characteristic under consideration, so that all tests that are intended to measure that characteristic will yield similar orderings of the same individuals.

3. The test must provide an evaluation of the same psychological characteristic throughout its range of scores.

4. The group (or groups) on which descriptive statistics are based should be appropriate to the test and to the purpose for which the test was designed and intended. This is a matter that will bear particular emphasis, since a norms population is meaningful and therefore useful *only* to the extent that it has been defined carefully. In some instances, as in the case of achievement tests in specific subject areas which are not uniformly offered or taught in precisely the same way, the problem of defining the norms population is not easy. A population must be chosen for which not only the subject of the test but the test itself is appropriate; and *appropriateness* is itself a concept that is frequently hard to define and keep distinct from the concept of *difficulty*.

5. Finally, data should be made available for as many distinct norms populations as there are populations with which it is useful for an individual or a group to be compared.

One might add to these a sixth point, namely that the items for the test itself should have been selected on the basis of data for samples drawn from the population for which the test is intended—that is, the group or groups for which norms will be given.

In addition, the population (or populations) defined and chosen as the basis for a set of norms should be homogeneous, in the sense that the individuals are all clearly members of it, and, in the case of educational tests, logical or even actual competitors for the same goals or rewards (e.g., accepted and enrolled freshmen in colleges of engineering). Similar considerations, incidentally, apply to the *use* of norms. The choice of the appropriate group with which to compare an individual should be made on the basis that it is useful and reasonable for the individual to be compared with its members. Obviously, because of differences that exist from group to group, a given individual may have as many different percentile ranks as there are groups with which he is compared. Thus, while his score on a test may be regarded as the *measurement* of his level of talent and is represented by a single fixed number (except, of course, for errors of measurement), his percentile rank is not fixed but represents an *evaluation* of his talent and will naturally vary depending on the normative group with which he is being compared. Therefore, it behooves the user, when he wishes to evaluate an individual's performance, to choose the normative groups with care and with an awareness and understanding of the differences among them.

Also, it is plain that the size of the norms group, in terms of both the number of schools and the number of students, and the design of the sampling procedure must be carefully worked out in order to maximize the precision of the norms and to minimize their bias.

Finally, the manner in which norms are presented should follow from the purpose or use for which the norms are intended. A number of different types of normative data are discussed later; for the present it will be sufficient to say that norms are most commonly presented in the form of percentile (sometimes referred to as mid-percentile) ranks. The percentile rank for each score is calculated quite simply by counting up the total number of examinees scoring below the score interval in question, adding to that number half the number in the interval, and dividing by the total number of examinees.

Types of Norms

National norms

The most general and most commonly used type of norms is the *national norms,* appropriate to the educational and age level (or levels) for which the test is constructed. One of the problems in defining the national norms group arises from the large number, variety, and complexity of the characteristics of students, as well as of schools and communities, that are correlated with and relevant to test scores. The variables that are associated with the characteristics of students include educational level, age, sex, race, present or intended field of study, socioeconomic level of parents (educational, occupational, and economic determinations), and sometimes, for achievement test norms, the aptitude test scores of the students. The variables that are associated with the school may include size of school, type of support (public, independent, and religious), pupil-teacher ratio, per pupil expenditure, curricular emphasis, and proportion of students who are college bound. Beyond this, the significant variables include region (for example, South versus non-South), type of community (i.e., rural-urban-suburban, or size of geographical area served by the school, or population density), socioeconomic level of the community, presence or absence of—or size of—a community library, etc. Davenport and Remmers (1950) made a study of sociological and economic characteristics by state and found a multiple correlation of about .96 with mean scores on qualifying tests for World War II A-12 and V-12 college training programs. R. L. Thorndike (1951) and Mollenkopf (1956) conducted similar studies at the community level and found much lower multiple correlations, ranging from about .45 to about .65. Thorndike offered some hypotheses to explain the differences between his results and those found by Remmers and Davenport, but in any case it is clear that community variables represent an important set of factors to consider in the construction of norms. To a limited extent it is possible to stratify on these variables, that is to say, to define homogeneous categories or strata on the variables and to sample appropriately within the categories. Occasionally, when the categories are sufficiently distinct and also meaningful to the user it may be helpful to provide *differentiated norms* separately by category. Thus norms are sometimes available separately by region, by sex, by type of school support, by type of community (urban-rural), and, of course, by educational level.

Schrader (1960) has pointed out that national norms have the distinct advantage of being simple, definite, and unique. National norms also have the advantage that, to the extent that publishers succeed in providing truly precise and unbiased national norms, it is possible to achieve score comparability across the tests of different publishers. On the other hand, the availability of a single norms table tends to obscure the fact that a percentile rank is not unique but represents only one of many possible evaluations of a test score. Furthermore, national norms may frequently be too general to permit specific action. Clearly, the more specific and, of course, the more relevant the norms group, the easier it is to make appropriate decisions based on test scores. Ideally, there should be as many norms tables as there are types of decisions to be made. However, as valuable as they may be for detailed decisions, one of the problems of providing many sets of differentiated norms (in addition to the substantial costs involved) is that the user is frequently confused by the wealth of information available to him and yearns for the simplicity of a single norms table.

Local norms

Although it is unquestionably the responsibility of the test publisher to make available the kinds of norms that are appropriate for the uses he claims for his test, in many instances the most useful kind of norms are the *local norms* collected by the user himself and based on students enrolled in his own institution. These norms have the advantage of homogeneity, since the students included in the norms all come from the same educational and social milieu and constitute a group with which the test user has first-hand knowledge and familiarity. Further homogeneity may be effected by separating the total group into finer subgroups that differ from one another in important and relevant respects.

Local norms are especially valuable when they are collected in a way that will permit the formation of particular decisions—for example, in the identification of students who would benefit from special instruction or in separating a total class into homogeneous subgroups for whom the instructional pace can be more clearly defined. The data that help to make such decisions are those that relate one set of scores to another, as in local studies of growth; or those that relate aptitude test scores to achievement, as in the construction of expectancy tables (described below); or those that relate test scores to individual or group characteristics, as in the preparation of *differentiated local norms,* for example by sex, by curriculum, or by intended major field of study.

Age and grade equivalents

In general, there are two kinds of normative, or reference group, comparisons (Lindquist & Hieronymus, 1964). One kind of comparison makes use of a *single* reference group and describes the standing of an individual's score in relation to the distribution of scores for that group. This type of reference is exemplified by the percentile distributions mentioned above and also by the normative scales described in the previous section on scaling. The second kind of comparison makes use of the mean scores on a *series* of reference groups and essentially identifies the group whose mean score is most nearly like the score under consideration. This approach is exemplified by *grade equivalents,* which are appropriate for subject-matter achievement tests highly dependent on the curriculum and on the grade in which the subject is taught. It is also exemplified by *age equivalents,* which appear to be more appropriate for such measures as general aptitude and intelligence which are less highly dependent on the curriculum.

The principal limitations of age and grade equivalents are those that have already been discussed in the previous section on scaling (pp. 20-21). Most of these limitations result from: (*a*) the fact that the equivalents are intended to represent an "equating" of age or grade level with performance on a test with which the age or grade level is imperfectly and nonlinearly correlated; and (*b*) the fact that age or grade level is *differently* correlated with different subject-matter tests. The imperfect correlation between age or grade and test performance leads to a number of anomalies, ambiguities, and inconsistencies that impair the usefulness of the age or grade equivalents. This is unfortunate

44

because, except for these defects, "equivalents" (which, it should now be clear, are *not* equivalents at all) appear otherwise to have the ideal characteristics of interpretive data—clarity, definiteness, and direct meaning. Additional difficulties with these equivalents arise from the fact that they can lead to absurd conclusions, for example: John has a grade equivalent of 6.3 in arithmetic skills when, in fact, John is only in third grade and has never been exposed to the arithmetic skills normally taught in sixth grade. Somewhat related to this kind of absurdity is the problem of assigning a mental age to a child for a level of performance that—because the curve of age versus performance flattens out in midadolescence—is not average at *any* age.

Another factor that contributes to the confusion surrounding these equivalents, particularly grade equivalents, is the variation from one community to another and even more, from one period of time to another, in the customs regarding the promotion of children through the grades. When promotion is based primarily on achievement, as it was in the early part of the twentieth century, the correlation between performance and grade level tends to be higher. When promotion is based primarily on age, the correlation between performance and grade level is lower. Grade equivalents derived under these two sets of conditions are not comparable (Gulliksen, 1950, p. 291).

Norms by age and grade

A kind of normative data that makes use of the relationship between test performance and age (or grade), but avoids many of the problems associated with the equivalents, is the *age* or *grade norms*. These data are essentially nationally representative percentile rank distributions, differentiated by age or grade. Instead of age or grade *equivalents,* they yield the usual kind of percentile rank that describes the person's relative standing in relation to other individuals who are of the same age or in the same grade. Unlike the equivalents, they make clear to the user just what the dispersion is within each age or grade group (that is, error of estimate in the bivariate plot of performance vs. age or grade), what the variation in dispersion is from age to age or grade to grade, and how the test score changes as a function of age or grade. Moreover, they do not permit the logically impossible statement that an individual stands at a level of development for which he has had no actual experiences. At the same time it should be pointed out that, like all norms for educational and psychological tests, changes in educational philosophies and customs will also render age and grade norms obsolete. Norms, including age and grade norms, collected at some prior time when the curricular emphases and methods of instruction were different from what they are today are simply not comparable with norms collected under present-day conditions.

It is important to note that the substitution of age and grade *norms* for age and grade *equivalents* effectively separates the function of norms from that of scales. Thus it is possible to develop a metric for a system of test forms and, entirely independently, to develop a collection of different kinds of norms—differentiated, for example, by grade, by region, by sex, by type of community, etc.—without committing the scale to any one of these sets of norms. The scale remains constant so long as the test is appropriate and relevant to the times. The norms, on the other hand, are free to develop and change as necessary to provide the particular interpretive information required at the time.

As has been pointed out, policies and practices regarding promotion have a direct bearing on the manner in which norms are prepared. Because of the custom, prevalent in the early 1900s, of promoting children to a higher grade only if their achievement warranted, it was typical for achievement test scores to show a higher correlation with grade level than they do today. It was also typical for the distribution of age for children in the same grade to be highly dispersed and positively skewed. In order to standardize the population within grade and at the same time to make it more homogeneous, some test constructors suggested the development of *modal age norms,* that is to say, grade norms for children of approximately the same age. While this procedure certainly helped to clarify and standardize the norms considerably, one of the problems associated with it was that the actual modal age group varied from one community to another, depending on local practice with respect to age at school entrance and also depending on local policies with respect to promotion. However, this problem, it is fair to say, was equally characteristic of norms to which the modal age concept and technique were not applied at all. Thus, while it may have been possible to collect data nationally on which to develop a system of modal ages in grades, it was quite possible that the modal age in grade for a given community would differ from the national norm to a degree that would affect the usefulness of the test norms in that community.[9] One method of developing modal age-in-grade norms was the system of *ridge route*

[9]This state of affairs, it is noted, applies to norms for educational tests generally, since such norms necessarily reflect educational practices. Therefore, to the extent that educational practices vary throughout the country, the problem remains that no single set of national norms would be entirely appropriate and applicable in a particular community. This condition would argue for the superiority of local norms that are assembled by the test user himself, who is familiar with and understands the local educational customs and can control his data accordingly.

norms developed by Kelley (1940), which involved taking the 12-month range in each grade that showed the heaviest concentration of ages and considering this age range as the modal age group for that grade.

The effect of basing grade norms on such modal age groups was to free them to some extent of the influence of the local practices of retardation and acceleration, to move in the direction of greater homogeneity and precision, and to produce a modal age group for each successive grade level that was usually one year older than for the previous grade. An additional effect, as would be expected in view of the typical positive skew in the distribution of ages within grade, was to produce a modal age population slightly above average in intelligence, since it included only those students who started at the modal age and were regularly promoted. In contrast, at most elementary grade levels, the unselected grade group was below average in intelligence because it included a number of older students who had been held back (Flanagan, 1951).

In general, the practice of constructing modal age norms is not as common today as it was 30 to 40 years ago. Because of the current philosophy (and practice) that elementary school children should, in general, be advanced to the next higher grade along with others of their own age, the distribution of age within grade is now more homogeneous and further selection is less necessary.

Some of the difficulties with *age norms* (as distinguished from grade norms) appear to arise from the fact that they are often developed for tests in specific curriculum, or subject-matter, areas for which grade norms are probably more appropriate. As a result, they present special difficulties. Flanagan (1951) has pointed out four problems that are associated with age norms. For one thing, they ignore grade level and implicitly assume that it is the chronological age, not the grade level in which instruction was received, that is more relevant to performance. This is an assumption that is probably not warranted for tests that measure specific educational outcomes, although it may be for tests of general intellectual functions that are not explicitly taken up in the classroom. Secondly, it is often difficult to select a reasonably representative age group, even by testing in several successive grades. Thirdly, age norms assume that growth is even and regular throughout the year and the same during the summer months as during the school year. This, too, is very likely unwarranted for tests that are based on explicit educational outcomes. Finally, they do not apply very well for subjects that are not taught on a continuing basis, since this would mean combining into one distribution data for students who *have* had and students who *have not* had instruction in a given subject-matter area.

Item norms

Sometimes a teacher who has administered a standardized test to his class will want to prepare an item analysis, essentially a percent-pass figure for each item, based on the responses of his students in order to determine the particular areas in the curriculum that need additional emphasis or elaboration. The identification and evaluation of the items or item areas that present difficulties have to be made, however, on the twin bases of *norms as a standard of performance* and *norms as existing performance*. For the first of these bases, the teacher (or, more generally, the community school system) must have in mind the inherent difficulty of the concepts tapped by the items, their relative importance in the total context of the subject, and some realistic conception of how easily these concepts can be grasped within the limitations of the abilities of the students in his class. For the second of the two bases, the norms as existing performance, he needs to have a similar set of item analysis data for a large group of students whose educational goals and whose personal and social characteristics match those of his own students, ideally a group of students assembled in the local community or in his own classes over a period of time. The use of the subjective *and* the statistical evaluation will enable him to idenfity the sources of weakness in his students that require additional attention.

School-mean norms

The norms that test publishers customarily have made available to test users are norms based on the performance of individuals for use in the evaluation of individuals. Although this kind of use is the purpose for which they are likely to be used most frequently, norms data based on the performance of individuals sometimes also are used by teachers and principals in evaluating the *mean* performance of their students, as though the norms represented relative standing among other means. However, norms based on individuals are simply not appropriate for this purpose. The variability of scores for individuals is far greater than the variability of school means, in the ratio of about 2.0 or 2.5, to 1 (Lindquist, 1930; Lord, 1959). Therefore, a school whose students average higher than the mean of the norms will be underevaluated, since the average performance of those students will appear to be less superior than it actually is. Similarly, a school whose students average lower than the mean of the norms will be overevaluated, since their performance will appear to be less inferior than it actually is. In recent years, test publishers have taken to publishing *school-mean norms* to serve the purposes of the schools that want to compare their own means with the means of other schools (Cooperative SCAT Series II Handbook, 1967;

Lindquist & Hieronymus, 1964). Since the school is typically the unit of sampling in preparing test norms, it is a fairly simple matter for the publisher to construct a distribution and, from it, a table of percentile ranks based on the means themselves. An additional advantage of these school-mean norms is that they make clear to the user how large a sample of schools was actually used in the preparation of the norms, a piece of information which is particularly significant and informative in view of the manner in which norms samples are typically selected. Since the school is the unit of sampling, the stability of the norms depends heavily on the number of schools sampled as well as on the number of students. Like general norms, the value of school-mean norms can be greatly enhanced if they are further differentiated in terms of school and community variables. However, differentiated school-mean norms will be possible only when the total norms program is large enough, as in the case of a program of the size of Project Talent (Flanagan et al., 1962), in which 1,353 schools were sampled, to permit the presentation of sufficiently large subsamples of schools to be meaningful.

User-selected norms

Sometimes the norms that are provided by the publisher, differentiated by region, type of control, type of student body, etc., do not satisfy the various purposes for which a school or college wishes to examine data. Occasionally a college will wish to compare itself with other colleges which it regards as its competitors for the same applicants. For example, a college located near a metropolitan area where there are, say, six or seven colleges, all different in curriculum, type of control, selectivity, etc., may nevertheless be interested in knowing how its students compare with the other five or six. One highly selective liberal arts institution may wish to compare the scores of its applicants with the scores of applicants to another highly selective, but *technical,* institution in the same city or in the same state, perhaps because it feels that they are both drawing from essentially the same applicant pool. Sometimes these insitutions manage to exhange their data individually and directly. Sometimes the test publisher can make available to the test user who requests it a combined distribution for the students enrolled at certain institutions specified by the user. It would be customary under these circumstances for the publisher to specify some minimum number of institutions for such a norms group in order to protect the anonymity of the individual institutions as well as to guard against excessive sampling errors, and also to specify the manner in which the students were selected to represent each institution. In general, since normative comparisons can have highly specific purposes, it also may be desirable to develop some systems of norms, in addition to those that are conventionally prepared today, that are based on sociometric clusters of institutions, i.e., institutions whose officials feel that they have something in common apart from the groupings that may be imposed on them by virtue of their formal characteristics.

Special-study norms

In general, norms are useful to the extent that the reference group is meaningful to the user. The national norms group is an obvious example of one such group. Differentiated norms, which further specify the strata within the national norms group, are also useful, perhaps more so than the national norm, for the same reason—they describe the behavior of homogeneous groups of individuals who have characteristics that are known and meaningful to the user. Local norms have the same characteristic; they are particularly well known and familiar to the user and are most useful to him for that reason. Similarly, a valid case can be made for norms that are *not* based on a random or representative sample of some defined population, but are based on *all,* or virtually all, the students in a well-known segment of the total population: e.g., all enrolled freshmen at the "Seven Sister" colleges; all ninth-grade students in the particular communities of Grosse Pointe, Shaker Heights, and Newton; all third-graders in the disadvantaged areas of Philadelphia. The special-study norms capitalize on the familiarity to test users of certain well-known groups of students and, in a manner of speaking, yield as much information about the sensitivity of the test and its ability to differentiate within both high- and low-scoring groups of students as it does about the groups themselves.

Norms that yield "direct meaning"

In order to make test scores meaningful, various techniques have been sought, either to describe the scores in terms of the performance of general groups (as in the case of national norms), in terms of the performance of more specific groups (as in the case of differentiated norms), and in terms of highly familiar groups (as in the case of local, user-selected, and special-study norms). All of these types of norms, however, are statistical and provide meaning only through the definition or familiarity with the group used as a basis for the norms. Ebel (1962) has maintained that the essential meaning of a student's performance is lost when it is said that he performs better than some particular percentage of his peers, unless it also can be specified precisely just what it is that he can do better than they. Ebel therefore suggested that the test in question be given "content meaning." He proposed that the test be illustrated by a short—say, a 10-item—test of highly discriminating items representative of the test to be normed. The items in the short test would be reproduced in detail for the test user to examine, so he could become familiar with their content, and therefore—since they would be a miniature representation of the full test—indirectly familiar with the content of the full test. Then, for students earning each of certain selected scores on the full test, a distribution of scores would be made on the short test. The user would then observe the modal score on the short test for each of the selected scores on the full test, and with the knowledge he would then have of the content of the short representative test, he would have a better idea of the meaning of the different scores on the full test.

Another type of content meaning suggested by Ebel derives from the ability to reproduce the universe of content from which the test items are drawn. Thus, the meaning of a raw score on a vocabulary test is derived from the fact that the items of the test are drawn in a specified random fashion from a specified source.

A third type of normative data that yield direct meaning is one that is described under the heading *expectancy tables* (p. 60). For each of a series of specified scores on the test (say, here, an achievement test), a distribution of course grades is given. Then, just as they are able to do with the content norms just described, the test users can observe the modal course grade and the dispersion of grades corresponding to each of the available scores on the test. In this way, the test scores acquire meaning in terms that are already available and familiar to the test users—on the scale of course grades that they themselves customarily assign to students. If the grades are assigned independently of the test, these data, which would normally emerge from a validity study, can later serve as guidelines in defining ranges of scores that would be equivalent to, or would merit, a grade of A, B, C, etc. Thus validity data can be made useful in two ways: first, the data on grades lend meaning to the scores on the test; and second, after meaning is established and after the user develops familiarity with the test as an independent instrument, the process is frequently reversed and the data on the test can be used to help objectify and standardize the assignment of course grades.

Functional interpretations

Test scores can also be made meaningful in terms of the student's ability to perform tasks of known difficulty. This kind of score interpretation is one which would permit statements like: A student who earns a score of x on the French test can read a French newspaper with comprehension. A student who earns a score of y on the mathematics test can solve problems in differential equations. A student who earns a score of z on the economics test understands the principal of marginal utility. The value of this kind of interpretation is that it appears to describe test performance in *absolute* and familiar terms that are easily transmitted and understood. However, like other types of score interpretation that appear to yield direct and immediate meaning, these functional descriptions are not quite so simple and clear-cut as they may seem. These descriptions imply, for example, that knowledge and understanding (e.g., of marginal utility), or ability and proficiency (to read French with comprehension or to solve differential equations), can be complete and absolute and can be described at a single standard or level of excellence. The use of these functional descriptions in the manner described fails to recognize that there are many degrees of ability to perform a real-life task. (The principle of marginal utility, for example, can be "understood" at many levels of sophistication.) These descriptions also fail to recognize the differences in difficulty that are inherent even in a task that appears as common and familiar as the task of "reading a newspaper." Clearly, there are many kinds of newspapers with many kinds of literary styles, each one representing a different kind and level of difficulty. There are also differences in difficulty between one type of written material and another, even within the same newspaper.

Although the interpretation of test scores by means of functional descriptions is by no means a straightforward, uncomplicated task, it is a way that merits additional study. Very likely it would involve a psychophysical scaling of various levels of accomplishment of tasks that are *apparently* familiar to the test user and the formation of a distribution of scale values for these tasks for selected scores on the test—much in the way that has already been described for the miniature test proposed by Ebel and for the course grades described in the preceding section.

Quality ratings

In a manner similar to that described for the short test, the course grades, and the functional descriptions, distributions of test scores can be made for each of a series of quality ratings that are customarily given to the students by the test users, ratings such as outstanding, excellent, good, fair, and poor or for a series of administrative judgments and courses of action like those implied by the descriptions high honors, honors, pass, and fail. As before, the value of referring the test scores to these ratings lies in the assumption that the ratings are familiar and meaningful to the user, and reasonably reliable. If these conditions do not hold, then the test scores will fail to acquire the desired meaning, or will fail to acquire stable meaning, or both.

It may bear repetition that while the various kinds of ratings described here will help initially to bestow meaning on the scores, it is almost inevitable that, as the test in its various alternate forms continues to be used, the metric for the system will gradually acquire its own meaning to a point where the role of the test and the role of the ratings are reversed and the *test* becomes the instrument to bestow meaning and stability on the *ratings*.

In each of the "direct meaning" types of score interpretation there is necessarily a *bivariate distribution* or *scatterplot* of the test score versus the rating (or versus the miniature test). Therefore, as would be true of any scatterplot, and as was also true of age versus performance and grade level versus performance, there is not *one* regression but *two*. In the preceding discussions the test score was uniformly taken as the independent variable, and the evaluations that resulted were the average scores on the "meaningful" variable (the miniature test, or the course grades, functional descriptions, or judgments and ratings) for selected scores on the test to be normed. But as in the case of age and grade versus test score, the regression could just as easily have gone in the other direction. The evaluations might have resulted in the average *test score* for each score on the "meaningful" variable. The fact that the interpretations are not unique would argue for presenting them in more than one way. For example, the fact that two regressions exist is evidence, of course, that the correlation between the "meaningful" variable and the test score is not a perfect one. This is so largely because the "meanings" themselves are likely to be highly unreliable and variable. The same consideration applies to the miniature test which, it is noted, would very likely be much less reliable than the very test for which it is being used as a criterion of meaning. This is not to say that such evaluations are not useful. However, as Ebel himself has suggested (1962), they are most informative if, in addition to the modal values on the "meaningful" variable for each array of test score, the entire scatterplot is given. In this way, the user can see directly what the degree of relationship is between the test score and the criterion.

One way out of the dilemma of the regression lines is to develop a line of comparability[10] between the two variables by the equipercentile method, or by an explicitly linear method if the results of the equipercentile equating turned out to be essentially linear. This type of procedure would yield ranges of scores corresponding to course grades of

[10]Described in the section on equating and calibration and in the section on comparable scores.

A, B, C, etc., to quality designations of outstanding, excellent, good, etc., for example, or to scores on a short test. These ranges would have the advantage of not depending on the direction of regression. However, as described in the paragraph that follows, these ranges of scores will not necessarily be unique with respect to the set of data and might therefore have to be determined anew for each set of data.

It would be expected, particularly in the case of the course grades and in the case of the judgments of quality and administrative action, that there would be some real and systematic differences in the regression system between one group and another, say, between one college and another. Obviously, the demands of quality and the criteria by which quality is judged will be quite different at a highly selective institution than at a community college whose purpose it is to provide educational opportunities for all secondary school graduates who apply, irrespective of ability level. For that reason, the "meaning" that emerges from a study of the relationship of test scores and judgments will not be general but will differ, depending on the group of individuals who make the judgments of quality and also depending on the group for whom the judgments are made. For this reason determinations of "meaning" have to be made locally and applied locally.

Additional ways of making scores meaningful could include procedures for constructing some of the nonnormative scales described in the scaling section of this chapter. Scores on the test could be attached to various levels of accomplishment by means of the judgment of experts who would be asked for their estimate of the minimum score that they feel would permit the designation of passing, honors, or high honors, or the designation of outstanding, excellent, good, etc. As indicated above, these techniques might well serve initially to give the test meaning but might later come to serve the opposite role, of giving the judgments themselves more rigor and precision.

Score differences

Although the most common types of norms are those that have already been discussed, there are other types of norms or, more generally, other types of interpretive data for tests. Some of the particularly interesting, and at the same time, troubling and difficult kinds of interpretive data are those that deal with score differences. Two such kinds of data—*growth* data and *over- and underachievement* data—are discussed here, not necessarily because they have originated in the same psychological context, but because they have many of the same methodological problems in common.

Growth—Although the measurement of status is indispensable for most of the purposes for which tests are used, it is also frequently important to make an assessment of growth. Considered in their simplest terms, growth measures involve the determination of status at the beginning and again at the end of the period of time in question. However, certain fundamental requirements must be satisifed before a determination of growth can be made. First of all, it is self-evident that the tests given at the beginning and end of the period must clearly be measures of the same function; otherwise, growth measurement is not possible. Secondly, the two tests (or better, the two test forms) must be expressed in the same units; that is to say, the test scores must be equated before the observation can be made that change has taken place. If not, then it will be possible to make the rather awkward observation that an individual, or indeed the average for an entire group of individuals, has dropped from the first to the second occasion when, in fact, everyone has improved his performance. This can easily happen if the second form is noticeably more difficult that the first. Even if the forms appear to have been equated, the careful investigator will do well to protect his data from the sampling errors of equating—which exist, of course, as they do in any statistical process—by dividing his total group into two random halves and administering the forms in the order X-Y to one half and in the order Y-X to the other half. There is an additional problem. Unlike physical measurement, where the effect is frequently either negligible or nonexistent, the very act of administering an educational or psychological test often produces a measurable change in the individual. Therefore a third requirement is that some careful controls need to be instituted to distinguish *growth*—which would be defined as an increment in score associated with the passage of time—from *practice*—which may be defined as an increment resulting solely from previous exposure to the test (that is, when little or no time has elapsed since the first testing, except as necessary to overcome the possible effects of, say, fatigue or boredom).[11]

One highly disturbing characteristic of score changes is their extremely low reliability. This may be explained by saying that the error of measurement of a score difference is essentially the *sum* of the errors of measurement of the two scores that go to make up that difference.

[11]There are many other problems involved in the measurement of educational growth, some of them clearly beyond the scope of this work but thoroughly treated in a rapidly growing literature dealing with the theory and methodology of score change, for example, in articles written by Lord (1956; 1958), McNemar (1958), Manning and DuBois (1962), Thorndike (1966), Tucker et al. (1966), and in a series of articles edited by Harris (1963), where there is also an extensive bibliography on the problems of score change.

(More precisely stated, the variance error of a difference between two independent scores is the sum of the variance errors of the component scores.) Since the errors on two independent tests are uncorrelated, there is no third subtractive term in the variance error of the difference to attenuate it. On the other hand, the variance of a difference score is not twice the variance of the component scores but something considerably less. If the two component standard deviations are equal, then the variance of the difference equals $2s_x^2(1-r_{xy})$, where x and y are the component (pretest and posttest) scores. Indeed, the higher the correlation between pretest and posttest scores, the smaller is the variance of the difference. Finally, when the reliability of the difference score is computed, the proportion of score variance attributable to error is quite substantial. For example, if the average reliability for the two tests is .90 and the correlation between them is .85, then, applying the formula given by Gulliksen (1950) for the reliability of the difference in scores on tests X and Y, when $s_x = s_y$,

$$r_{dd} = \frac{\bar{r}_{xx} - r_{xy}}{1 - r_{xy}},$$

the reliability of the difference score is .33. Clearly, it would be very unusual for the reliabilities of score differences between two parallel measures to be high, since the test-retest (alternate-form) correlation, r_{xy}, will generally be almost as high as the average reliability, $\bar{r}_{xx}$. In general, low reliabilities will occur unless, as Lord (1956) has pointed out, a very long period has intervened between the two testings or unless the trait measured is subject to rapid changes over time. Because of the highly unreliable nature of score differences, it is extremely easy to get a distorted picture of gain scores for individual score interpretation. (*Mean* score differences for groups of individuals, however, would be expected to be much more reliable, the more so for larger groups.) A preferred interpretation would invoke making an estimate of the *true* gain, as derived by Lord, for example, rather than interpreting the observed gain literally.

Although the assessment of growth data is vital to the successful conduct of educational research, the problems of interpreting those data are sufficiently numerous and complex that investigations in this area should not be undertaken casually. Anyone seriously interested in conducting studies involving score changes would be well advised to make a thorough examination of the methodological literature first.

Over- and underachievement—It has always been hoped that the use of appropriate measures in education would make it possible to identify those students whose potentially good performance was being adversely affected by other factors not related to ability. Once these students were identified, it would be a logical next step to determine the nature of these other factors and to take steps to correct them.

In order to carry out this type of educational diagnosis and cure, it was thought necessary to administer two kinds of tests—a test of intelligence, or "innate" ability, and a test of achievement. The difference between an individual's scores on these two tests would then be taken as an indication of the extent to which his achievement in school was falling short of his ability. Today, educators are far less certain that there is a clear distinction between ability and achievement, just as they are less certain today of the distinction between nature and nurture, concepts that very likely led to the formulation of *ability* (or *aptitude*) and *achievement* as separate and separable entities. In any case, it has become clear that the conceptual distinction between measures of aptitude and measures of achievement is not always a sharp one, and so the distinction is often made operationally—for example achievement tests consist of items that are closely dependent on the material explicit in the curriculum (e.g., geography, trigonometry, American history, etc.); aptitude tests do not.

At the time when the distinction between ability (or aptitude or intelligence) and achievement was thought to be a real distinction—also at the time when test scores were more frequently expressed in the form of quotients than they are today—the degree of over- or underachievement exhibited by a student was sometimes described in terms of the AQ. However, this index is subject to all the problems already discussed in connection with age norms and age equivalents in addition to which is the fact that it is highly sensitive to methodological and sampling differences in the development of the educational age and mental age indexes. A variation of the AQ, suggested by Cureton (1937), was the ratio of the observed educational age to the educational age expected of that individual on the basis of his mental age. The expected educational age was defined as the average educational age for all individuals with a given mental age.

Often the concepts of over- and underachievement become semantically troublesome. While it was reasonable to conceive of an individual who was, so to speak, working below his potential, the question was sometimes asked, how is it possible to achieve *beyond* one's potential? The term *potential* seems to imply a physiological limit that, by definition, cannot be exceeded. Without attempting to resolve these logical difficulties, the research in this area more recently has simply addressed itself to the question of accounting for the discrepancy between *actual* and *predicted* achievement. In a review of the problems of design of studies of over- and underachievement, R. L. Thorndike (1963) observed that the whole problem of over- and underachievement may be thought of as essentially the problem of errors of prediction, and he offered the following reasons for these errors:

1. Errors of measurement, or unreliability, both in the predictor and in the criterion.

2. Heterogeneity in the criterion variable; i.e., errors of prediction result from the intermingling of two or more subgroups, each evaluated on a continuum that is *ostensibly* the same for all subgroups but actually different. (Thorndike gave as an example of criterion heterogeneity the case of two groups of students, one coming from a college where the marking system is strict, the other coming from a college where the marking system is lenient. Errors of prediction arise from the fact that the As, Bs, Cs, etc., from the two colleges have been combined as though they have the same meaning. Either the criterion variable should be adjusted for its different meaning in the two groups or the groups should be analyzed separately.)

3. Limited scope in the predictors, i.e., not all of the relevant determiners of the criterion variable have been studied. Thus, a person's performance may differ from expectation only because of the investigator's failure to establish the expectation appropriately.

4. The unpredictability of the events that intervene between prediction and outcome—uncontrollable variations in the quality and type of instruction, exposure to different kinds and amounts of remedial teaching, and patterns of educational, vocational, and personal guidance. Moreover, "chance" events occur in an individual's life that cannot be predicted and cannot be assessed even if they could be predicted.

5. Unmodifiable characteristics in the individual's nature or background—e.g., sex, race, socioeconomic status, parents' educational level; and the customs, attitudes, and opportunities for intellectual stimulation both at home and in the community.

6. Personal and educational factors that *are* subject to modification and manipulation. (As Thorndike has pointed out, these are the areas that represent the main focus of research concern in the work on over- and underachievement. These are the areas in which it is wished to identify the relevant factors and their interrelationships, if a modification in these factors will produce desired changes in the criterion.)

7. Finally, a source of error, which Thorndike discussed in a separate context, is "criterion contamination." Examples of criterion contamination are: (*a*) the "Hawthorne effect"—the improvement (or impairment) in the criterion measure simply as a result of the individu-

al's awareness that he is a subject in the experiment; (*b*) direct "coaching" on the criterion test, or more generally, an effect on the specific criterion score, positive or negative, that is not a reflection of a general effect in the individual; (*c*) a bias in the subjective judgment of the individual who assigns a rating on the criterion measure. (*d*) An additional type of criterion contamination, distinct from the above three and not discussed by Thorndike, comes about when the criterion rating has been affected, consciously or unconsciously, by the rater's prior knowledge of the individual's score on the predictor. Sometimes, only the rater's evaluation of the criterion performance is influenced. Sometimes, when, for example, the rater is also the instructor, his knowledge of the predictor score may influence his *treatment* of the individual, and this in turn may influence the individual's actual criterion performance (an effect which has been referred to as the "self-fulfilling prophecy"). Both types of contamination nearly always will have the effect of producing a high correlation between predictor and criterion.

The methodological problems involved in the study of over- and underachievement are similar in many ways to the interpretation of score gains, since, like score gains, the discrepancy between criterion and predictor also represents a *difference score*. For example, like the score gain, the discrepancy between actual and predicted achievement is extremely unreliable. Also, the biasing effects of regression are just as prominent in studies of over- and underachievement as they are in studies of score gains. The selection of high and low groups on the predictor will *necessarily* result in the (fallacious) identification of "underachievers" and "overachievers," since individuals who are high scoring on the predictor are likely to be lower scoring on the criterion and since individuals who are low scoring on the predictor are likely to be higher scoring on the criterion. That is, the method of the study *coerces* the result of the study. For the same reason, the definition of over- and underachievement in terms of the difference between comparable scores on predictor and criterion will not work; high-scoring individuals on the predictor are generally lower scoring on the criterion and will therefore show small or negative differences; and low-scoring individuals on the predictor are generally higher scoring on the criterion and will therfore show large differences. The *only* kind of discrepancy score that is unbiased in this respect is the difference between the actual achievement for an individual and the achievement that is estimated for him on the basis of his standing on the predictor.

Sometimes the study of the relationship between predictor and criterion reveals the fact that there are different kinds of relationships for different subpopulations and that a moderator variable is required to account for the differences. For example, it is possible that while scores on the various scholastic aptitude tests that are currently in use are highly predictive of college success for white students, they are not so highly predictive for black students, or that the slope and intercept of the regression line are different for black and white students. Generally, however, when the same regression system applies equally well for all subgroups, it is common practice to operate on the discrepancy between actual and predicted achievement in an effort to reduce it.

Aside from the possible confusions that may result from the use of the terms "overachievement" and "underachievement," it may be quite useful to examine the possibility that a student is performing as well, or perhaps better, than he would be expected to do on the basis of his performance on some predictor variable. For this purpose the discrepancy score between actual and expected performance is the score to use. However, because of the unreliability of such differences it would be advisable to consider as significantly over- or underachieving only those individuals whose discrepancies are clearly extreme. Similarly, also because of the unreliability of differences, it would be advisable to consider as those who have gained or lost significantly from pretest to posttest only students whose *true score* gains or losses are extreme.

Expectancy tables

A highly effective way to examine a student's record for discrepancy between aptitude and achievement scores—indeed, between any two scores or evaluations—is to prepare expectancy tables of criterion scores for fixed values on the predictor variable. These tables are essentially scatterplots of predictor versus criterion, or, from another point of view, norms on the criterion variable, differentiated by score on the predictor variable. For each score or score interval on the predictor, a percentile rank distribution of scores on the criterion variable is formed, showing the percentage of cases scoring at and below each chosen score on the criterion variable. Thus, as in all sets of differentiated norms, criterion performance is evaluated, but only among individuals who are homogeneous with respect to their performance on the predictor. Frequently the percentages given in expectancy tables are the proportions of individuals earning the same score on the predictor who earn a criterion score *as high or higher* than the score indicated.

Sometimes expectancy tables are prepared by generating, as an approximation, idealized normal distributions, one for each score interval on the preditor variable X, using actual data only to calculate the predicted criterion scores Y and the standard error of estimate. These values are taken, respectively, to be the means ($M_{y \cdot x}$) and the standard deviation ($s_{y \cdot x}$) of the Y arrays and are used in conjunction with tables of the normal ogive to determine the percentage of cases falling at and below (or at and above) each criterion score in each of the Y arrays of the table.

The construction of expectancy tables is very simple, constituting merely an extension of the usual norms distribution. However, their very simplicity makes them especially effective in displaying validity data and in making evaluations of over- and underachievement. Nevertheless, care should be exercised in these evaluations that the distinction between prediction and criterion is a clear one, separated either by an intervening period of time between the two determinations or by an unmistakable difference between the functions measured in the two determinations. If this condition is not met, if it is not clear which measure makes the promise and which yields the fulfillment, then the notion of achievement-relative-to-a-baseline is necessarily confused and meaningless.

Profile charts

Some of the comparisons that are made in the interpretations of an individual's (or a group's) test scores are the comparisons with an arbitrary but relevant *standard* of performance. Others, very likely the most common types of comparisons, are the normative or the *interindividual* comparisons, those that are made against the existing performance of a relevant reference group. Still others, like studies of growth and studies of over- and underachievement, involving the comparison of two or more scores obtained by a single individual, are the *ipsative* or *intraindividual* comparisons. Unlike *normative* comparisons, which are taken from a series of measurements, each administered to a member of a group and evaluated in terms of their departure from the mean of the group, *ipsative* comparisons are taken from a series of measurements, all administered to one individual and evaluated in terms of their departure from the mean of the individual. Ipsative measurements—a term apparently originated by Cattell (1944)—are of value in the field of counseling and guidance where it is considered important to know, for example, which of various occupational careers an individual is most interested in pursuing or in which of various aptitude and achievement areas he shows relative strengths and weaknesses. Ipsative measurements also would be important in identifying those areas in which the individual needs special additional instruction or remedial help.

The device that is most often used for intraindividual comparisons is the *profile chart*. This is essentially a graphic representation of a system of comparable scores on a series of tests on which an individual's various scores are plotted. The construction of the comparable score scales requires that the series of tests be normed in advance, all on the basis of a single well-defined and *relevant* group of individuals, and converted to a scale with the same system of numbers and yielding the same distribution shape (frequently normal) for all tests. The evaluation of performance itself is in fact normative *as well as* ipsative, since it involves a determination of the configuration of the individual's scores and a comparison of the scores relative to one another and, also, a comparison of the individual scores and the configuration of scores against those of the norms group.

One of the principal difficulties with the individual profile chart is the fact that it depends on the evaluation of differences among scores for an individual. Since the reliability of such score differences is ordinarily low, the usefulness of generalizations based on such differences is frequently questionable.

A second difficulty is that interpretations of profile charts depend on the particular method of scaling employed. If the tests are scaled in terms of grade equivalents, for example, an individual whose scores are equally high relative to the reference group in social studies and arithmetic may nevertheless have two different grade equivalents in this group—say, 8.4 in social studies but only 6.2 in arithmetic. This difference in grade equivalents is largely the result of the difference in the correlations of the two tests with grade level; the within-grade dispersion in social studies is likely to be larger than the within-grade dispersion in arithmetic.

The comparison of an individual's profile chart with the flat profile of a group on a series of tests is a normative comparison, analogous, in some sense, to the comparison of an individual's score with the distribution of scores for a norms group. There is, however, an important difference. A norms distribution displays the dispersion in the group and permits the placement of the individual in a particular rank position relative to that group. The profile chart, on the other hand, permits only the simple observation that the individual's profile is different from the group's profile (which is, by definition, a straight line connecting the 50th percentile points across all the tests). It does not permit an evaluation of the *degree* of departure of the individual's profile chart from the aggregation of profile charts for the members of the reference group. The flat profile of the reference group may indeed represent the profile of not a single member of the group and may be quite different even from the modal profile in the group. A more defensible approach to the problem of comparing profiles than the use of the profile chart would involve the definition of the individual's position as a point in *n-*

dimensional space and the determination of the relative departure of that point from the n-dimensional centroid.

Technical Problems in the Development of Norms

There are at least two principal sources of inaccuracy in a normative evaluation, say a percentile or percentile rank. One of these, the error of measurement, arises from the imprecision of the test and the testing process. The other arises from the inaccuracies of the sampling procedures and in the data used in developing the norms themselves. (Still other inaccuracies are inherent in the statistical procedures and in the data used in scaling and equating the scores.) These two sources of error may be considered to be additive, in the sense that the variance error in the determination of an individual's percentile rank involves the sum of the variance errors corresponding to the two sources of inaccuracy. However, the two kinds of error operate differently. Errors of measurement for individuals are a function of the testing process and may be thought of as independent of one another. As such they tend to cancel out for individuals when considered in the aggregate and vanish as the size of the group increases for which a normative evaluation is sought. The error in the norms, however, is a different matter. While this error also depends on the size of the group, it is the group used in *developing the norms* that determines the error, *not* the group for whom the evaluation is sought. Thus once the norms are determined, the error, which may have been considered random at the time of sample selection, now remains in the norms in the form of a bias and is transmitted *equally* to all evaluations of a given score, whether it is an individual's score or the mean score for a group even of a thousand individuals or more. In this sense, it behaves like the error of equating, discussed later in this chapter, which depends in part on the size of the sample *used* for determining the conversion equation. But once the error becomes part of the conversion equation, it remains fixed and permanent and independent of the size of the group for whom the mean score is converted to the scale for the other test. If the group used for developing the conversion is separate from the group used for norming, then the variance error of the normative evaluation of a converted score is the sum of the *three* sources of variance—the test, the norms, and the equating. The error in the evaluation is also, of course, a function of the *level* of the score, since each of the three types of error varies with score level.

Sampling

Cornell (1960) has pointed out that sample statistics lack precision when: (*a*) the errors of random sampling are large, i.e., when there is a wide dispersion of the distribution of the sample statistic about the population parameter; (*b*) when there is a bias, e.g., when the mean of all such sample statistics and the parameter are not the same; and (*c*) when the observations themselves are inaccurate or incomplete.[12] Although the sampling frame in general should be so designed as to minimize random errors and to avoid entirely systematic errors (bias), it is sometimes the better strategy to accept a small bias if by doing so it also is possible to reduce the random errors susbstantially. The essential measure of error is the sum of squared deviations about the parameter, and whichever procedure yields the smallest value for that sum is the procedure to follow.

Since the usefulness of decisions that are based on statistical data depends heavily on an accurate assessment of the error in the data, it is extremely important to develop a plan for the collection of the data for which the error is known or at least can be approximated. There are a number of samples for which the error is unknown:

1. A sample of convenience—one that happens to be easily available. Samples of convenience will almost certainly be biased. They will more often be taken from schools that are easily accessible by conventional modes of transportation, larger and therefore helpful in building up the size of the norms sample, better known and therefore more likely to be brought to mind, more innovative and progressive, more willing to try out new ideas (as in testing), more cooperative and willing to be known as "forward-looking" institutions that have participated in a "national survey" or "study" and therefore more easily available, and less likely to be embarrassed by the performance of their students. These characteristics, needless to say, are associated with higher test scores.

2. A sample based on an outdated list or on a list that does not adequately cover the target population—for example, a list of secondary schools that includes only those under public control and not private and parochial schools.

3. A sample with a high proportion of nonresponse or nonparticipation.

4. A "pinpoint" or "representative-area" sample—for example, the purposive selection of individuals or groups or clusters of individuals (e.g., classes, schools, or communities) that are thought to be "typical."

5. A "quota" sample, in which the primary sampling unit—e.g., the state or region—is selected by an appropriate sampling plan, but in

[12]The author wishes to acknowledge the valuable assistance provided by the outline and, in many instances, the particular phrasing used in Cornell's excellent overview of sampling. The following pages describing the various types of samples and sampling procedures borrow heavily from his treatment of this topic.

which the choice of the specific community or school is made by the test publisher's regional representative or salesman according to general guidelines that are defined for him in advance. For example, he may be instructed to choose two large urban schools, one suburban school, and one rural regional school in a defined region, but will be permitted to choose the specific schools himself. The problem here, of course, is that, within the limits of his authority, he will very likely choose a sample of convenience.

6. A sample that is selected on the basis of expert opinion. For example, a number of educators, presumably knowledgeable in their field, assemble a list of schools that in their judgment represent the target population.

In all of these procedures there is likely to be a bias, either because the sampling frame itself is biased, because the participants are self-selected and by definition biased, or because conscious nonautomatic choices are likely to be made on the basis of insufficient knowledge or on the basis of conscious or unconscious predilection. Nor does the danger of bias exist only with respect to the mean. It is frequently overlooked that bias can and does exist with respect to variability. "Typical" samples, for example, are likely to have less variability than random samples.

Finally, there are samples that have subtle biases, sometimes because the sampling procedure itself is biased and therefore inappropriate, sometimes because the samples are drawn from biased populations. Samples that contain such biases are those that are dependent on occasionally implicit (and incorrect) assumptions—for example, that surname initials are uncorrelated with ability, that birthdates are equally frequent and also uncorrelated with ability, that telephone subscribers or owners of television sets are a random segment of the population, and so on.

Unlike the foregoing methods of selecting samples, there is a class of sampling procedures called *probability sampling,* which, if carried out properly, does permit the objective evaluation of error. The characteristics of probability sampling are: (*a*) the process of selecting the individuals or elements in the sample is not left to the judgment or convenience of the investigator but is automatic; (*b*) each individual (or primary element) in the sample has an equal, or at least *known,* probability of being selected in the sample; and (*c*) the weights used to compensate for disproportionate representation in the sample are derived from these probabilities and are used in the estimation of the population parameters.

There are various methods of selecting random samples. Most often, in large norms or sample survey projects, these methods are used not singly but in combination. The simplest method is the *unrestricted* or *simple random* sampling method, which involves the selection of a group of individuals of size N in such a way that each individual has the same probability of being selected, and every possible combination of N individuals has the same probability of being selected. One way to accomplish this is to assign to each of the individuals in the population a unique serial identification number and to select the individuals for the sample from a table of random numbers. When the population is much larger than the sample, as would be true of most norms projects, the individuals may be drawn from the population pool without replacement. Otherwise, either replacement is necessary—which would mean that the same individual could appear in the sample more than once—or care should be taken to use standard error formulas that are appropriate to selection from finite populations. While the unrestricted random sampling procedure is simplest conceptually, it is nearly always extremely difficult administratively and much more costly to execute than its precision warrants. In most instances, equivalent precision can be achieved much more economically by other methods of sampling.

Stratified random sample—A modification of the unrestricted random method which effectively introduces greater precision into the results is one that first divides the total population into relatively homogeneous *strata* on the basis of one or more variables that are correlated with the variable in question (i.e., test score). For example, it is not uncommon, in sampling for norms, to stratify on the basis of region, type of school (public, private, religious), and size of school. Once the strata are established, the sampling within strata is conducted by the method of simple random sampling. The allocation of sample sizes to the strata leads to a more stable estimate if the sampling units are allocated among strata in proportion to the total number of units in the strata. If the allocation of sampling units is far from optimum, then it is possible for the stratified sample to have a sampling variance even greater than that of a simple random sample of the same size. Generally, efficiency in stratified sampling is achieved by taking proportionately larger samples in strata that are larger, more variable, and cheaper to sample.

Stratified sampling, which capitalizes on the relationship between certain variables and test score, tends to enhance the reliability or the precision of the norms. If the multiple correlation (R) of the stratification variables with test score is known for the unit of sampling—e.g., the school—then the variance error, $SE_{\bar{x}}^2$, of the mean of the norms group is approximately:

66

$$\text{SE}_{\bar{\bar{x}}}^2 = \frac{s_{\bar{x}}^2}{k}(1 - R^2),$$

where k equals the number of schools in the norms sample and $s_{\bar{x}}^2$ is the variance of observed school means. Thus, if a particular level of precision is achieved by simple random sampling of k schools, then that same level of precision can be achieved with only $(1 - R^2)k$ schools if the stratified sampling method is employed. If R is about .55, as R. L. Thorndike (1951) and Mollenkopf (1956) found for community variables, then only 70 percent as many communities would have to be used with stratified sampling methods as would be necessary if the communities were sampled entirely at random from the population.

Systematic sampling—The first step in drawing a *systematic*, or *spaced, sample* of size m from a population of M elements is to divide the list of M elements into m successive blocks or subgroups of size c (where $c = M/m$) and, starting at a random element in the first block, to select every cth element. If the listing of the M elements in the population is random, then systematic sampling is essentially equivalent to simple random sampling. However, if the blocks are sufficiently homogeneous, i.e., if the variance within blocks is smaller than the variance between blocks, then systematic sampling is more precise than random sampling and resembles stratified sampling. For example, if the elements of the list are students and the students are arranged in order of test score, then a systematic sample automatically stratifies by test score. If the elements of the list are schools and the schools are grouped by geographical region, then a systematic sample automatically stratifies by region.

The principal advantage of the systematic sample is its simplicity, and, of course, the fact that, if the list is arranged in homogeneous categories with respect to a variable that correlates with test score, it will be a stratified sample. The danger in a systematic sample is that it may have unwittingly been drawn in phase with an unsuspected periodicity in the ordering of the population. To take an obvious example, if a population of children is ordered: boy, girl, boy, girl, etc., then a systematic sample of every cth individual, where c is an even number, will result in a sample of all one sex. To guard against this possibility it is advisable to construct a list of m random numbers and to select according to a *different* random number in each of the m blocks. If the blocks previously have been arranged in a stratified fashion, then this procedure will yield a strict stratified-random sample.

Cluster sampling—Very seldom, if ever, are norms samples selected with the individual student as the unit of sampling. To carry out such a selection, e.g., at one grade level in a city, it would be necessary to assemble a list of all the students at that grade-level in the entire city and draw a random sample without regard to the school or the class within the school. The result of such a sampling effort would be that perhaps two students would be drawn from one class in a school, three from another class in that school, one perhaps from a class in a second school, none from other classes in that school, etc. Clearly, for reasons of administrative convenience and economy alone, it is far better to take a "natural" group, or *cluster,* of individuals, such as the school or the class within the school, as the unit of sampling. In addition, such selection would be less disruptive of the school's program and undoubtedly less disturbing to the students who are selected. Moreover, data collected for entire classes and schools would be more useful at a later time to both the students and the schools and would form a better basis for research.

For these reasons norms samples nearly always have been chosen with the school as the unit of sampling, a procedure that is quite proper and certainly reasonable under the circumstances. However, probably because of their failure to appreciate fully the significance of the fact that sampling error is a function of the method of random sampling, test publishers in the past have tended erroneously to estimate the standard error of their norms samples as though the students in their samples had been drawn individually and at random from the total student pool. It happened also that, by choosing the school as the unit and testing exhaustively in the school, as would be the preference of the school officials, it was easy for test publishers to build up the total sample size to what appeared to be quite respectable proportions. The result was that their assessment of the precision of their norms was deceptively high, and this encouraged them to continue to use an insufficient number of schools for norms in the belief that the reliability of the norms depended solely on the number of individuals tested.

The distinction between the two kinds of variance errors—based on students and based on schools—may be described as follows: As a general principle the variance error of the mean of the entire distribution of a norms sample is a function of the variance of the scores (or means of scores) earned by the units of sampling divided by the number of such units. Thus, when the individual student is used as the unit of sampling, the appropriate variance error of the overall mean is given as:

$$\text{SE}_{\bar{\bar{x}}}^2 = \frac{s_x^2}{\sum\limits_i^k n_i} = \frac{s_x^2}{N}, \tag{1}$$

where s_x^2 is the variance of all the individual scores in the sample, k is the number of schools in the sample, and $\Sigma_i^k(n_i)=N$ is the sum of the number of individuals tested in each of the schools in the sample, i.e., the total number of individuals in the entire sample, On the other hand, when the school is used as the unit of sampling and there is no sampling of students within school, the appropriate variance error of the overall sample mean, assuming that all schools are of equal size, is given as:

$$\mathrm{SE}_{\bar{x}}^2 = \frac{s_{\bar{x}}^2}{k}, \qquad [2]$$

where, as before, $s_{\bar{x}}^2$ is the variance of observed school means. Now if the students in each school represented merely a random sample drawn from the entire pool of students, then (leaving aside the variations in school size) equations 1 and 2 would be equivalent. The fact is, however, that the aggregation of the samples of students in all the selected schools does *not* represent a random sample of students selected from the entire population of students. There are marked differences among schools. Lord (1959) estimated that the standard deviation of school means is about four-tenths the size of the standard deviation of individual scores. This would represent a significant intraclass correlation and indicate that the school does indeed represent a homogeneous "cluster." Earlier Lindquist (1930) called attention to the same fact and argued strongly that because of the great variation in *school* achievement relative to the variability in achievement of individual students, the practice of emphasizing mere *size* of the norms sample was fallacious. When the school is used as the sampling unit, it is the number of *schools* as well as the number of *students* that determines the reliability of the norms. Lindquist (1966) also pointed out that the ratio of the variability among schools relative to the variability among students appears to be a function of the subject matter, with greater ratios associated with subject-matter areas in which the opportunity to learn what is tested is relatively restricted to the classroom.

To illustrate the fact that equations 1 and 2 give quite different results, it may be helpful to consider some fictitious but reasonable data and to observe the results of applying the two equations. Say that a norms administration has been conducted in a random sample of 256 schools ($k=256$) tested at the 12th-grade level, where the number of students (N_i) averages about 100. Assume that the test has been standardized on all 25,600 students and that the scores have been converted to a scale on which the standard deviation for all students combined is 10. Say further that Lord's estimate holds here and the standard deviation of school means is 4. According to equation 2, then, the appropriate standard error of the mean of the norms sample (ignoring the variation in school size) is $4/\sqrt{256}=.25$. If equation 1 had been used (inappropriately) here, the standard error of the mean would have been calculated as $10/\sqrt{25,600}$, or .0625, a standard error one-fourth as large as it should be. In order to achieve a standard error of .25 by random sampling of students, only $(10)^2/(0.25)^2$, or 1,600, students would have had to be tested instead of 25,600—one-sixteenth the actual number. The ratio of the numbers of students that are required under the two methods of sampling to reach the same level of precision is known as the *efficiency* of simple random sampling of students relative to cluster sampling of schools. (It is understood, of course, that this is only *statistical* efficiency. In spite of the greater statistical efficiency of simple random sampling, it is generally more efficient from an adminis-trative point of view to use cluster sampling for norms.)

There are additional distinctions and refinements, not only the design of the sampling procedures but also in the assessment of the reliability of the norms. Equation 2, for example, is appropriate for cluster sampling when testing is exhaustive in each cluster and when all clusters (or schools) are of the same size. When the schools vary in size, as they inevitably do, then according to Lord (1959), the variance error of the mean of the norms, as given in equation 2 should be modified, as follows:

$$SE_{\bar{\bar{x}}}^2 = \frac{s_{\bar{x}}^2}{k}(1 + C_N^2).$$ [3]

Equation 3 is a convenient approximation to the desired variance error in which $C_N = s_N/\overline{N}$ is the coefficient of variation of school size. Therefore, to use, for illustration, data collected by Mollenkopf (1956) in a sample of 426 10th grades: if s_N, the standard deviation of school size (i.e. the size of the 10th grade in a school) is 91 and $\overline{N}$, the mean of the school sizes, is 108, then $1+C_N^2=1.71$, adding 71 percent to the size of the variance error represented by equation 2. As a result of this modification it should be clear that if the variation in school sizes relative to mean size given in the illustration is typical, then *about 30 times as many cases would be necessary in exhaustive cluster sampling to achieve the same reliability of norms as would be achieved by simple random sampling*. One can then judge the extent to which the reliability of norms can be misrepresented by the simple but inappropriate use of the size of the total norms sample as a measure of the reliability.

Frequently it is convenient and desirable to do successive sampling, for example to sample schools as the primary unit and, once the schools have been selected, to sample students *within* schools. Such a plan would be called *two-stage* sampling. The variance error appropriate to two-stage sampling would contain two separate additive terms, each appropriate respectively to the two separate types of sampling. Sometimes the sampling is a multistage process. For example, the principal unit of sampling may be the community. Then schools may be sampled within community, classes within schools, and finally students within classes. Just as for two-stage sampling, there would be a separate additive error term in the formula for the variance error of the overall mean, each term identified with the variance error for the corresponding stage in the sampling process.

In general, two-stage sampling *at least* is required for most norming projects. It is appropriate, in fact highly useful, in reducing the excessive sampling errors that are characteristic of cluster sampling, when, for example, two or more tests are to be normed simultaneously for the same population. Under these circumstances, the appropriate procedure is to select the schools first and then, assuming that the time limits and oral instructions permit, to administer each of the tests to a random fraction of each class. The best practical procedure for accomplishing this is to package the test books for each of the, say five, tests in the order a, b, c, d, e, a, b, c, d, e, a, b, etc., and to distribute them in this way in each classroom, thus automatically drawing simultaneously five systematic random samples. (As cautioned above, care should be taken to avoid the possibility that the method of drawing this sample will be in phase with a periodicity in the seating arrangement in the classrooms.) The great advantage of this procedure over the procedure of selecting a different set of schools for norming each test is that it maximizes the number of schools—the significant factor in the error of cluster sampling—in each of the five norms samples. Moreover, since all five tests are normed on random samples, all drawn in the same way and all in precisely the same schools, the variation among samples attributable to differences among schools is eliminated. It should be pointed out, however, that this greater comparability highlights the need for taking special care that the sampling of schools be planned and conducted in such a way as to avoid bias; for any errors in the sampling here will be reflected in the norms for all the tests.

It is probably advisable for tests that are normed in two or more grades to be administered to the students (or to random samples of the students) in all such grades in all schools in the norms sample. Otherwise, if the sample of schools selected for each grade is independently drawn, then the progression of means in the population from each grade to the next will not be reflected in the sample data. Although rare, it will even be possible for students in the norms sample at a higher grade to earn a lower mean score than the students in the norms sample at a lower grade—purely as a result of random fluctuation—and this is more likely to happen if the grade-to-grade differences are small. While it is true, of course, that random selection of schools tends to give protection against such inversions, it often happens that the characteristics of the sample are so disturbed by the refusal of some schools to participate in the norms program that when the norms data are finally assembled the sample is no longer random as originally intended. In these circumstances, score inversions between grades can be the result. The procedure of testing the students in all the grades in all the schools sampled for norms will introduce a grade-to-grade correlation across schools, thereby reducing the standard error of the difference between grade means and consequently reducing the likelihood of an inversion in the relative order of the means in successive grades. For the same reason—to reduce the standard error of the difference between means of successive grades—it is advisable, in constructing norms for successive grades that necessarily cut across schools—norms for grades 4–12 for example—to test the entire succession of grades in each of the communities sampled, taking care to provide continuity by finding the feeder schools whenever possible for each of the schools at the higher grade levels.

In general, the purpose of the sampling procedure is to ensure that each individual in the population stands an equal chance of being selected for the norms sample. Three two-stage sampling procedures will be described to accomplish this. In each procedure the first stage will involve the selection of schools, and the second will involve the selection of students.

1. In the first method, schools are drawn at random from the total pool of schools, each school standing the same chance with each other school of being drawn for the sample. With this kind of sampling arrangement the distribution of school sizes, for example, will approximate the distribution of sizes in the population, and it is appropriate therefore to test the same fixed *proportion* of students in each school. If that proportion is 100 percent, then, of course, there is no error for sampling within schools and the variance error of this sampling procedure is the same as that given in equation 3. If the proportion drawn in each school is less than 100 percent (but the same in each school), then the variance error of the entire two-stage sampling process is given by the equation:

$$\text{SE}_{\bar{\bar{x}}}^2 = \frac{1-f}{kf\overline{N}}\,\overline{S_x^2} + \frac{1}{k}(1 + C_N^2)s_{\bar{x}}^2, \qquad [4]$$

where $\overline{N}$ is the average school size, f is the proportion of the students tested in each school, and $\overline{S}_x^2$ is the arithmetic mean of the within-school variances for the norms population (Lord, 1959). Table 2, from Lord (1959) and based on Mollenkopf's (1956) data collected at grade 6 and, also, at grade 10, demonstrates how sampling within schools can produce economies in the numbers of students required for testing. For example, given a standard deviation of individual scores of 10, a standard deviation of school means of 4, a mean school size $(\overline{N})$ of 58, and a value of C_N (the coefficient of variation of school size) equal to .55, only *nine* percent of the number of students that would be required for exhaustive (100 percent) sampling within schools would be needed if a random sample of only *two* percent in each school were actually chosen for testing (grade 6 data). If $\overline{N} = 108$ and $C_N = .84$ and if only a random *one* percent of the students in each school were tested, then the total number of students would need to be only *four* percent as many as would be required by norming procedures in which all the students are tested in each of the schools chosen for the norms (grade 10 data). It should be added, however, that while the numbers of students required for norms

TABLE 2

Efficiency of Two-Stage Sampling Procedures for Sixth-Grade Data and for Tenth-Grade Data

	Subsampling Proportion* (f)	Number of Schools Needed in Sample (k)	Portion of Error Variance Attributable to		Standard Error of Mean of Norms Distribution (Equation 4)	Expected Number of Examinees Tested $(kf\overline{N})$	Ratio of Number of Examinees $(kf\overline{N})$ to Number Required with Usual Cluster-Sampling Method
			First Stage of Sampling $\frac{1}{k}(1 + C_N^2)s_x^2$	Second Stage of Sampling $\frac{1-f}{kf\overline{N}}\overline{S}_x^2$			
6th Grade Data	1.00**	36.0	.579	.000	.76	2088	1.00
	.50	38.5	.541	.038	.76	1116	.53
	.25	43.5	.479	.100	.76	632	.30
	.10	58.5	.356	.223	· .76	339	.16
	.05	83.5	.250	.329	.76	242	.12
	.02	158.5	.131	.448	.76	184	.09
10th Grade Data	1.00**	36.0	.758	.000	.87	3888	1.00
	.50	37.0	.738	.021	.87	1998	.51
	.25	39.1	.698	.060	.87	1056	.27
	.10	45.2	.604	.155	.87	488	.13
	.05	55.5	.492	.266	.87	300	.08
	.02	86.3	.316	.442	.87	186	.05
	.01	137.6	.198	.560	.87	149	.04

*The impossibility of fractional students is ignored.

**This row represents the usual type of simple cluster sampling.

Note: Reprinted from Lord, 1959, with permission of *Journal of Experimental Education*.

are shown in both illustrations to be dramatically reduced as a result of the sampling within schools, this saving is achieved at the expense of increasing the number of schools from which the students are drawn—in the first illustration by a factor of 4.4; in the second illustration by a factor of 3.8.

2. In the second procedure, schools are again drawn at random from the total population of schools, with each school standing the same chance of being selected. If a *fixed number* of students are selected from each school, instead of a fixed proportion, it would be necessary to weight the frequencies for the larger schools proportionately more heavily than for the smaller schools. The variance error of the mean of the norms for this norming procedure is given in the equation:

$$SE_{\bar{x}}^2 = \frac{1}{nk}\left(1 + C_N^2 - \frac{n}{N}\right)\overline{S_x^2} + \frac{1}{k}(1 + C_N^2)s_{\bar{x}}^2, \qquad [5]$$

where n equals the fixed number of students tested in each school (Lord, 1959). Here too the economies of sampling within school are dramatic but not quite as dramatic as if the number tested within each school were proportionate to the size of the school.

3. In the two procedures discussed thus far each school has the same probability of being selected for the norms sample. In the third, the likelihood that a school would be chosen is proportional to the size of the school. Once the school is chosen, the number of students is held fixed; the same number of students is tested in each school, irrespective of its size. That this method of selection gives each student in the population the same probability of being selected for the sample as every other student may be demonstrated by considering the joint probability of the two selection procedures. Under this plan of selecting schools, each school has the probability N_i/N_t of being selected, where N_i is the number of students in the school and N_t is the number of students in the population. With a fixed number of students to be tested from each school, the probability that an individual student from a school will be tested is n/N_i. The product of these two probabilities, n/N_t, indicates that the likelihood that a particular student will be chosen is independent of the school he is attending and is the same for all students.

A practical and effective way of sampling schools in proportion to size may be described thus:

1. List the schools in the population (or, if stratified sampling is being conducted, in the particular stratum of the population) in any convenient order and indicate the number of students in each school.

2. For each school determine a range of numbers: the lower of the two numbers in the range is obtained by summing the numbers of

students in all the schools that precede it in the list and adding one; the higher of the two numbers is obtained by summing the numbers of students in all the schools that precede it in the list and adding the number of students in that school. That is, determine the cumulative enrollment figure for all schools preceding and including each listed school.

3. Choose k numbers (k equaling the number of schools to be selected) from a table of random numbers, no random number to be larger than the total number of students in the population.

4. For each random number identify the school with the range of numbers within which that random number falls. (If, in this process, the school is identified twice, it should be drawn twice and appear twice in the sampling of schools. For the second stage of sampling, then, it would be appropriate to draw two subsamples of students independently—i.e. with replacement—from the school.)

The variance error of the two-stage sampling plan in which the probability that each school is selected for the sample is proportional to its size and in which the number of students selected from each school is fixed is given in the equation:

$$\text{SE}_{\bar{\bar{x}}}^2 = \frac{1}{nk}\left(1 - \frac{n}{\overline{N}}\right)\overline{S_x^2} + \frac{1}{k}s_{\bar{x}}^2, \qquad [6]$$

in which it is assumed that school size is unrelated to school achievement and to within-school variance (Lord, 1959). If these assumptions can be satisfied, then the sampling error given by equation 6 is seen to be clearly smaller than that given by equation 5. However, if the assumptions underlying equation 6 are *not* satisfied—if the large schools generally have larger within-school variances or larger between-school variances than the small schools—then the sampling variance of equation 6 may turn out to be larger than that of either equation 4 or 5.

As was pointed out earlier in this section, it is advantageous, from the point of view of improving the precision of the sample, to stratify on the basis of variables that are related to test score. However, upon examination of equations 3, 4, and 5, it is clear that the variance error of the norms also can be reduced by reducing the variation in school size (that is, by reducing the value of C_N). In other words, the error in the norms can be reduced by stratifying on school size, even though school size may be unrelated to test score. Once the schools are grouped into strata that are relatively homogeneous by size, sampling can be carried out independently in each stratum by any one of the three procedures already described, after which the frequencies for each of the strata would be appropriately weighted to approximate their representation in the population. From a purely intuitive point of view this procedure is eminently reasonable since it ensures that the relatively rare large schools will be adequately sampled. No such result is assured without stratification on size.

The variance error of the mean of a norms sample, drawn by stratifying the norms population on one or more dimensions, is given as:

$$\text{SE}_{\bar{\bar{x}}}^2 = \frac{1}{\left(\sum_h K_h N_{i_h}\right)^2} \sum_h K_h^2 N_{i_h}^2 \cdot \left[\frac{1 - f_h}{k_h f_h N_{i_h}} \overline{S_{x_h}^2} + \frac{1}{k_h} s_{\bar{x}_h}^2\right],$$

where K_h is the number of schools in stratum h in the population; k_h, N_{i_h}, f_h, S_{x_h}, and $s_{\bar{x}_h}$ are, respectively, the values of k, N_i, f, S_x, and $s_{\bar{x}}$ for stratum h. It is assumed in this equation that school size is constant within stratum and that the proportion of schools in each stratum used in the sample is small.

Although the present discussion of sampling procedures has been written as though the second stage of sampling normally involves the selection of students at random from each school, the practicalities of the real situation often militate against this. Administrative constraints in the schools below the college level may permit the random selection of *whole classes* within schools but not ordinarily the random selection of individual students. In schools that operate under the educational philosophy of homogeneous grouping, these classes represent *clusters* of students in the accustomed sense of the term; they should not be regarded as representing random samples of individuals drawn at large from the school.

School-mean norms

The use of school-mean norms was considered on p. 48. A major disadvantage of the procedure of sampling within schools is that it does not provide the mean score for all the students in each school but only for a sample of them. Moreover, since the obtained means are derived from subsamples of the students in each school, they necessarily will be more dispersed than would be the means based on all students in each school. In order to make it possible to provide school-mean norms, an estimate is therefore needed of the variance of the means of the k schools assuming *all* the students in each school had been tested. Such an estimate is provided by the equation (Lord, 1959):

$$\hat{s}_{\bar{X}}^2 = s_{\bar{x}}^2 - \frac{1}{k} \sum_i^k \frac{N_i - n_i}{n_i N_i} S_{x_i}^2,$$

where

$\hat{s}^2_{\overline{X}}$ = the estimate of the variance of the school means for *all* the students in the schools in the norms sample,

$s^2_{\overline{x}}$ = as before, the variance of the observed means,

k = the number of schools,

N_i and n_i = respectively, the total number of students in school i and the number of students tested in school i, and

$S^2_{x_i}$ = the observed variance of scores in school i.

With the value of $\hat{s}^2_{\overline{X}}$ available, it remains to use the ratio $\hat{s}_{\overline{X}}/s_{\overline{x}}$ as a scaling factor and to construct a frequency distribution of the means, $\overline{X}_i$, having the same general shape and overall mean as that observed for the distribution of $\overline{x}_i$ but with a standard deviation equal to $\hat{s}_{\overline{X}}$.

Size of tolerable error in norms

Once the mathematical relationships between the types and numbers of sampling units and the size of the resulting sampling error are clarified, the practical questions normally arise: How small should the error be? How many schools and students are needed for the norms? Unfortunately, these questions cannot be answered in the abstract. They obviously depend on a number of factors: the purpose for which the norms are intended; the importance of the decisions that would be based on the norms and their dependence on precision; the opportunities that would be available to reverse those decisions, once they are found to require correction; and the cost, in any sense of the word, of making the wrong decision as against the cost of increasing the precision. It should be remembered that the error of norms cannot be regarded in the same way as one would regard the error of measurement; it does not depend on the number of cases being evaluated and does not tend to vanish as that number increases. As indicated earlier in this section, once the norms are determined the error stays on in the manner of a bias and is just as prominent whether the score that is being evaluated is the score of an individual or the mean score for a large group.

Although definitive answers cannot be given to the question of maximum tolerable error in norms, some guidelines may be developed to aid in the consideration of sample size, based, as Lord (1959) has done, on expected differences between major subgroups in the population. Consider an example similar to the one he discusses, and say that one has separate norms for northern and southern schools. Suppose also that the true difference in means for the two subgroups is about 2.5 points in favor of the northern schools on a scale for which the standard deviation of scores for all students in the country is 10 points. Finally, suppose that

$s_{\bar{x}}$, the standard deviation of school means, is 4, that C_N equals .8, and, also, that there are about three times as many schools in the north as in the south. One might then ask: How many schools should be chosen from each region, with 100 percent sampling in each school, to give near certainty—say, at a confidence level of 99.5 percent—that the difference in means will not be reversed, with southern schools scoring higher than northern schools? According to equation 3 the variance error of the mean of the norms for the southern schools would be $(16)(1.64)/k$; the variance error of the mean of the norms for the northern schools would be $(16)(1.64)/3k$; and the variance error of the difference in those means (the sum of those two variances) would be $(4)(16)(1.64)/3k$. With the variance error of the difference fixed at 6.66 (the square of 2.58, which would correspond to the 99.5 percent level for one-tailed confidence) and the difference between means fixed at 2.5, 6.66 equals $[(2.5)^2(3)k]/[(4)(16)(1.64)]$ and k equals 37 (approximately). Therefore, 37 schools would be needed for the southern norms and 111 schools for the northern norms. Naturally, with different levels of confidence specified for the reversal in the means or with mean differences other than the one considered here, the number of schools required for the norms would be different. It should not be overlooked too that the error that was assessed here is the error in the mean. If, instead, one were to consider the error in the median, the standard error would be 25 percent greater than the standard error of the mean, implying that at the level of confidence specified one would need 56 percent more schools than one had counted on—about 58 schools in the south and 173 in the north. Moreover, the error in the norms would increase as one moves out to the tails of the distribution. At the 1st and 3rd quartiles the standard error is 1.36 times the error at the mean; at the 10th and 90th percentiles the error is 1.71 times the error at the mean; at the 5th and 95th the ratio of standard errors is 2.11; and at the 1st and 99th the ratio is 3.74.

In view of the size of the error in norms distributions, it is clearly advisable to take advantage of the techniques of multistage and stratified sampling in an effort to reduce the error. In order to prevent reversals in score of the kind just discussed it is advisable to test successive grades in each school, if grade norms are to be prepared. It is similarly advisable to test the same students at both times in the year, if spring and fall norms are to be prepared. In general, longitudinal norms, or a logical approximation to the notion of longitudinal norms—as, for example, testing in successive grades in the same schools, if the same students cannot be followed through the grades—are far preferable to cross-sectional norms, for which the standard error of the difference between grades is so much greater.

Beyond the general considerations that norms should be as precise as their intended use demands and the cost permits, there is very little else that can be said regarding minimum standards for norms reliability. Lindquist (1930) once suggested that the standard error of the mean of a norms distribution should be no greater than one-eighth of the standard deviation of school averages ($s_{\bar{x}}$). If $s_{\bar{x}} = .5s_x$, as he estimated, then the standard error of the norms (at the mean) would be one-sixteenth the standard deviation of individual scores. Then, 64 schools drawn at random from the population of schools, or 256 students each drawn at random from the population of students, would be needed to satisfy his suggested standard of norms reliability. When regarded in this light, it would not seem that such a standard is excessively high, especially in view of the fact that, with appropriate attention to the more sophisticated techniques of sampling, it is possible to increase the precision of norms without appreciably increasing costs.

Another rule for deciding on the maximum tolerable error in norms might be derived from the purpose of the test itself and its need for precision, which, in turn, should be reflected in the standard error of measurement of the test scores. A general consideration, suggested by R. S. Levine,[13] might be that the combined error at the mean due to error of measurement *plus* error in the norms should not be appreciably greater than the error of measurement alone (see also Cooperative School and College Ability Tests, 1967). Say, specifically, that the standard error arising from both sources of error combined should be no more than one percent larger than the standard error of measurement alone. Since the combined variance error is (approximately) equal to the sum of the variance errors in the components ($SE^2_{combined\ error} = SE^2_{meas} + SE^2_{norms}$), the standard error of the norms alone is found to be $(SE_{meas})\sqrt{(1.01)^2 - (1.00)^2}$, or $.14SE_{meas}$. By this rule, then, the standard error of the norms (at the mean) should be no more than 14 percent of the standard error of measurement. If, for example, the standard deviation of the distribution of scores is taken to be 10 and the standard error of measurement is 3.0 (test reliability equaling .91), and if Lindquist's rule, that the standard deviation of school means is $.5s_x$, is used, then by equation 2 the number of schools required for simple cluster sampling is about 142. If, instead, the standard deviation of school means is taken to be $.4s_x$, then the number of schools required is only about 91. It is clear that for less reliable tests the error of norms by the rule suggested here would be relaxed and the number of schools required for the norms sample would be correspondingly reduced. If the

[13]Personal communication, April 1967.

reliability of the test is .84 and the standard error of measurement $.4s_x$ and if the standard deviation of school means is taken at $.5s_x$, then the number of schools required for norms drops from 142 to about 80. With the same test reliability (.84) and a standard deviation of school means of $.4s_x$, the number of schools drops from 91 to about 51.

General Considerations in the Development of Norms

More fundamental than the numbers of students or the numbers of schools that are used for the norms is the consideration that the population be clearly specified in advance and that the sample be drawn with strict adherence to the rules for automatic and random selection. Otherwise, there is no guarantee that the norms will represent any particular population, and the considerations of error that have been discussed here—i.e., the considerations of random departures from a population parameter—will not apply. This is not to say that norms data that fail to meet these ideal conditions are not useful. They may, in spite of their bias, represent a close enough approximation to the ideal for most practical purposes. It is only that, in the absence of these conditions, it may not be possible to make an accurate assessment of the degree of bias in the norms or the size of their error.

One major problem in the development of norms (alluded to earlier) is the fact that many schools that are invited to participate in a norms administration will decline the invitation. If willingness to participate is correlated with score level, as may well be the case, then obviously the failure of a substantial proportion of the sample of schools to participate in the testing will bias the results.

There are various ways to help counteract this bias. One is to choose two or three times as many schools for the norms as are needed for each category of size, region, type, etc., and to resort to a random second or third choice within that category if repeated efforts to persuade a school to test are unsuccessful. Another, of course, is to try to make the testing as attractive and profitable to the schools as possible, by providing them with data on the performance of their students and relating those data to standard measures already in use. Finally, every attempt should be made to confine the lengths of the testing periods to the lengths of the class periods and, of course, to keep the amount of testing to a minimum. One way of accomplishing this, if more than one test is to be normed (and all tests require the same amount of testing time), is to follow the procedure suggested above, of randomizing the tests within each class-room so that each student takes only one test.

Another way of reducing testing time is to follow a procedure suggested by Lord (1962) for unspeeded tests that are scored simply for number right. In this procedure the total test is divided into random sets of items drawn at large from the total test. Each set of items is then administered to a random fraction of the total group. Lord reported in his study of this procedure that, from the data for each of the subgroups, he made separate estimates of the mean and variance for the full-length test and averaged them to yield a single estimate of the mean and a single estimate of the variance. These estimates then were applied to the formula for the negative hypergeometric distribution (Keats & Lord, 1962) to generate frequencies for the entire range of scores. The results of Lord's study indicate that high norms reliability can be achieved by administering fewer items to many examinees just as it can be achieved by administering many items to fewer examinees. Therefore, the procedure is especially useful in those situations where the cost of administration time, or the difficulty in obtaining it, is greater than the cost or difficulty in obtaining examinee groups. However, it should be cautioned that the procedure offered by Lord is not universally appropriate—for example when performance on an item is not independent of the context in which it occurs. This means, among other things, that it cannot be applied when there are items near the end of the test that are omitted because the examinees do not have enough time to attempt them. Also, although it is possible that this procedure of estimating norms can be extended to tests that are scored by other methods, at the present time it is appropriate only to those tests that are scored number right.

One of the persistent difficulties with norms, made most apparent in the concept of the national norm, is the fact that the samples chosen by the different publishers for their tests probably differ so that the norms are not directly comparable, despite the fact that they may all purport to be national norms. There are a number of reasons for this. One is that the test publishers may define the norms population somewhat differently, possibly with respect to the decision to include or not to include atypical subgroups (e.g., schools for retarded or disturbed children, schools for the physically disabled, schools for children in bilingual and bicultural areas, schools for delinquent children, etc.). Another is that different publishers will treat special problems of sampling in different ways (e.g., the problem of the nonparticipating school) with the inevitable result that various elements of bias will creep into the norms. And a third, of course, is the fact that norms will differ as a result of sampling error alone. Lennon (1964, 1966) has called attention to the problem of differences in the norms groups of different publishers and has urged that an anchor test be administered to norms groups in order to estimate the parameters of a single standard norms group for all tests. Two procedures for accomplishing this purpose suggest themselves, both involving the administration of an anchor test, say Test U, to the "standard" norms group (Group t) as well as to the norms group (Group α) of an individual publisher who is administering his test, say Test X, for norming. If it is assumed that the regression system of X on U is the same for Group t as for Group α—that is, that the standard error of estimate, the slope, and the intercept of X on U are the same for Group t as for Group α—then the following equations,[14] attributed to L. R Tucker (Gulliksen, 1950, chap. 19; Angoff, 1961a), can be used for estimating the mean and variance on Test X for Group t, the "standard" norms group:

$$\hat{M}_{x_t} = M_{x_\alpha} + b_{xu_\alpha}(M_{u_t} - M_{u_\alpha}),$$

and

$$\hat{s}^2_{x_t} = s^2_{x_\alpha} + b^2_{xu_\alpha}(s^2_{u_t} - s^2_{u_\alpha}).$$

Once these estimates are made, the frequencies for the entire distribution of Test X may be generated by means of the negative hypergeometric distribution (Keats & Lord, 1962) if Test X is scored for number right. Otherwise a normal distribution with the estimated mean and variance may frequently be taken to be a reasonably close approximation for most practical purposes.

Another procedure for estimating the frequencies of the distribution for the "standard" norms group is one that was suggested by Lord[15] and used by Levine (1958) in estimating the national norms for the College Board Scholastic Aptitude Test. This procedure is analogous to the procedure described in the preceding paragraph and derives from the same assumptions but deals with the frequencies of the distribution of scores instead of the mean and variance. Working with the scatterplot of scores on Test U versus Test X for the publisher's norms group, Group α, and dealing one at a time with each interval of score U_i on the distribution of Test U for Group t (the "standard" norms group), the ratio of frequencies, f_{i_t}/f_{i_α}, is calculated and then multiplied by each of the observed frequencies in the array for score U_i. When this is completed for the arrays for all values of U_i, there will be a new scatterplot of scores on Test U versus Test X estimated for Group t. At this point the frequencies are added across all values of scores on U to yield a total frequency for each score X_j. These frequencies, one for each level of score X_j, represent the estimated distribution on Test X for the

[14]The derivation of these equations is given in the section on equating and calibration.
[15]Personal communication, c. 1957.

"standard" norms group, Group *t*. Finally, this distribution may be smoothed by any one of the methods already described—with the aid of a French curve or spline, by the analytical method of a rolling weighted average of frequencies such as that described by Cureton and Tukey (1951), or, if Test X is scored number right, by the negative hypergeometric distribution developed by Keats and Lord (1962).

Within the past decade or two, there have been some noticeable improvements in the manner in which norms have been developed and reported. Probably the most significant developments have been noted in a fast-growing literature on the theory of sampling, especially as applied to norms development, and an accompanying awareness on the part of test publishers and investigators in general of the practical significance of these advances. For example, the painstaking efforts and care with which the sampling plan for Project Talent (Flanagan et al., 1962) was developed and executed is evidence of a sophistication in these matters that had not existed as little as 10 years previously. The development of the recent norms for the Lorge-Thorndike Intelligence Tests (Lorge et al., 1966) and for the Iowa Tests of Educational Development (Lindquist et al., 1966) also shows an attention to technical detail that has not been observed until recently. Lennon (1966) has pointed out too that the definitions and descriptions of the characteristics of the norms populations and the descriptions of the methods of sampling from those norms populations that are currently found in test manuals are more detailed, comprehensive, and technically advanced than they had been before. However, Lennon also pointed out, as had Cureton (1941) and Schrader (1960), that because of differences among test publishers in their definitions of the norms populations and in their methods of sampling from those populations, the percentile ranks for the "national" norms groups reported by various publishers were not directly comparable. Both Lennon and Cureton suggested as a solution to this problem the use of an anchor test that would permit establishing the comparability of different tests in terms of the same estimated national norms group. (Methods of estimating distributions with the use of an anchor test were described above.) Cureton also had suggested, as a solution to the problem of comparability of norms, the use of the concept of a standard group such as Toops' "Standard Million" (c. 1939). Toops had suggested that the characteristics of norms populations for the Ohio College Entrance Tests could be standardized and thus made comparable from test to test and, at the same time, made relatively homogeneous, by applying a series of restrictive or stratifying criteria whenever a norms sample was to be collected. However, it should be pointed out here that, although the use of restrictive criteria, such as those that Toops had recommended, would tend to make norms comparable over a period of time, they would not be equally representative of the population taking the test if the population changed. For example, Toops restricted his population to white students. While this restriction would not have excluded many black students from the norms populations 30 years ago, it would very likely exclude many more, even proportionately, today and very likely still more in years to come, as the proportion of black students enrolled in institutions of higher education increases.

3. Equating and Calibration

In most testing programs or test offerings it is manifestly advisable, for various reasons, to have multiple and interchangeable forms of the same test. However, since two forms of a test can rarely if ever be made to be precisely equivalent in level and range of difficulty, it becomes necessary to *equate* the forms—to convert the system of units of one form to the system of units of the other—so that scores derived from the two forms *after conversion* will be directly equivalent. If this is properly done, then, and only then, is it possible to say—after appropriate controls are considered—that there has been a change in a group's mean, say, from 20 to 25 points, after a period of special instruction (and perhaps as a consequence of it), even though the test forms administered on the two occasions were different forms. With equating properly executed it becomes possible to measure growth, to chart trends, and to merge data even when the separate pieces of data derive from different forms of a test with somewhat different item characteristics. It also becomes possible to compare directly the performances of two individuals who have taken different forms of a test. In a high-premium selection program, for example for college admissions or for scholarship awards, it is especially important for reasons of equity alone that no applicant be given special advantage or disadvantage because of the fortuitous administration of a relatively easy or difficult form of the test.

In adhering strictly to the concept of equating, a special point should be made of the notion that what is being sought is a conversion from the units of one form of a test to the units of another form of the *same* test, much in the sense that one thinks of a conversion from inches to centimeters, from pounds to grams, from Fahrenheit to Celsius, and so on. This notion implies two restrictions. The *first* is that the two instruments in question be measures of the same characteristic, in the same sense that degrees of Fahrenheit and Celsius, for example, are both units of temperature, inches and centimeters are both units of length, etc. In the case of the more common types of physical measurement this requirement is obvious. It makes no sense to ask for a conversion from, say, grams to degrees of Fahrenheit or from inches to pounds. Similarly, it makes little sense to ask for a conversion from a test of, say, verbal ability to a test of mathematical ability, or indeed across any two tests of different functions. This is not to say that it is inappropriate to draw a regression line relating two tests of different function, any more than it is inappropriate to regress, for example, weight on height. However, the problem of regression and prediction and the problem of transforming units are different problems. The latter is highly restrictive with respect to the types of characteristics under consideration; the former is not. The *second* restriction implied by the notion of equating is that, in order to be truly a transformation of only systems of units, the conversion must be unique, except for the random error associated with the unreliability of the data and the method used for determining the transformation; the resulting conversion should be independent of the individuals from whom the data were drawn to develop the conversion and should be freely applicable to all situations. Indeed, these two restrictions that are imposed on the concept of equating—that the characteristics measured by the tests be identical and that the transformation be independent of the groups of individuals used to develop the conversion—go hand in hand. For if the two tests were measures of different abilities, then the conversions would not be unique but would very likely be different for different types of groups. A conversion table relating scores on a verbal test to scores on a mathematical test developed from data on males, for example, would be noticeably and predictably different from a similar conversion table developed from data on females—owing to the fact that in our society men and women perform much more similarly on verbal material than on mathematical material. This issue of the nonuniqueness of conversion tables across different tests has been discussed in greater detail by Angoff (1966). However, suffice it to say here that equating, or the derivation of *equivalent scores,* concerns itself with the problem of unique conversions which may be derived only across test forms that are *parallel*—that is, forms that measure, within acceptable limits, the same psychological function. (The operational definition of parallelism that may be adopted here is essentially the one offered by Wilks [1946] and extended by Votaw [1948]: two tests may be considered parallel forms if, after conversion to the same scale, their means, standard deviations, and correlations with any and all outside criteria are equal [Gulliksen, 1950].) The problem of *nonunique* conversions of scores across *nonparallel* forms will be reserved for fuller consideration later in the discussion of *comparable scores.*

A commonly accepted definition of equivalent scores is: *Two scores, one on Form X and the other on Form Y (where X and Y measure the same function with the same degree of reliability), may be considered equivalent if their corresponding percentile ranks in any given group are equal* (Flanagan, 1951; Lord, 1950). Thus, if the two forms were sufficiently different in difficulty that the shapes of the distributions of raw scores for the same group of examinees were markedly different, the method of equating that would yield equivalent scores is one that would stretch and compress the scale of one form (say Form X) so that its distribution would coincide with the distribution of the other form (Form Y). As a consequence of this method of equating, an individual would earn the same converted score regardless of the form he took.

In general, the conversion of X scores to their equivalent Y scores will be curvilinear. If, for a given group of examinees, Form X is the easier form and Form Y the more difficult form, the equating of scores on X to scores on Y (X on the abscissa; Y on the ordinate) will yield a curvilinear conversion following the general shape of the scatterplot relating the two forms, i.e., concave toward the upper left. If Form X is the more difficult form and Form Y the easier form, then the conversion will similarly be curvilinear but concave toward the lower right. As another example, if Form Y gives a more platykurtic distribution of scores for a group of individuals than does Form X, the conversion, again following the general shape of the scatterplot, will be generally S-shaped. Finally, if the two distributions are of the same shape, differing in none of their moments beyond the second, the conversion will be linear.

By definition, successive forms of a test are constructed to be very nearly equivalent in all the important respects. Therefore, it is reasonable to assume that the shapes of the raw score distributions will be the same and that the conversion of X scores to Y scores can be accomplished simply by changing the origin and unit of measurement; that is, by adjusting only the first two moments. As was just indicated, this type of conversion is expressed in the form of a straight line. To correspond with the earlier definition of equating, the *equipercentile* definition, which stated that scores on two tests are equivalent if they correspond to equal percentile ranks, the definition for *linear* equating would state that scores on two tests are equivalent if they correspond to equal standard-score deviates,

$$\frac{Y - M_y}{s_y} = \frac{X - M_x}{s_x},\qquad [7]$$

which has precisely the same form as the equations for linear scaling $\{z_{c_\omega} = z_{x_\omega}$ or $(C - M_{c_\omega})/s_{c_\omega} = (X - M_{x_\omega})/s_{x_\omega}\}$ discussed on pp. 7–8. When the terms are appropriately rearranged, equation 7 takes the form, $Y = AX + B$, where $A = s_y/s_x$ and $B = M_y - AM_x$, A being the slope of the conversion line, and B the intercept (the point on the Y axis where it is intersected by the conversion line). It is important to emphasize that linear equating is a very close approximation to equipercentile equating when the shapes of the raw score distributions are similar. If one is prepared to assume that differences in the shapes of the distributions of raw scores on the two forms are sufficiently trivial so they may be disregarded, linear equating is to be preferred. Unlike equipercentile equating, it is entirely analytical and verifiable and is free from any errors of smoothing, which can produce serious errors in the score range in which data are scant and/or erratic.

There is little doubt that the only way to ensure equivalent scores when the distribution shapes are different is to equate by curvilinear (equipercentile) methods. Under such circumstances the equivalency is established by stretching and compressing the raw score scale of one of the forms so that its distribution will conform to the shape given by the other form. In some extreme instances the stretching and compressing is so dramatic that a difference between two adjacent converted scores in one part of the raw score scale may be seen to be as much as two or three times the difference between two adjacent converted scores in another part of the raw score scale. This is the expected result of equating two tests that differ greatly in their difficulty characteristics and is indeed inevitable if a system of equivalent scores is being sought that is independent of the characteristics of the particular test forms.

If, on the other hand, it is recognized that the raw score scale for a test reflects the inherent characteristics of that test—its level of difficulty, the dispersion of its item difficulties, and the intercorrelations among its items—and one wants the converted score scale for the test to reflect these characteristics, a model that permits a different kind of transformation of the raw scores may have to be erected. Suppose, for example, one is operating a testing program that is administered annually and is addressed to the same general level and range of examinee ability year after year. Suppose also that, as a result of administrative action, the purposes of the testing program are extended; say that the tests are now also to serve in the selection of scholarship winners. Because of this additional function it is now desired to make a variety of discriminations in the upper ranges of ability, even at the expense of some discrimination in the lower ranges. To accomplish this, harder tests are introduced and administered to the new groups of examinees. If the new forms are equated to the old ones by means of equipercentile equating, their scaled scores will be forced to conform with the scaled scores of earlier forms, and the fact that they have a higher ceiling than the earlier forms will not be reflected in their scaled scores. As a result of the equipercentile equating, then, the scaled scores for the very high-scoring examinees will tend to underrepresent their levels of ability; that is to say, such examinees will earn lower scaled scores than their abilities warrant, at a level approximating those of the less able examinees.

It therefore may be well to examine another model for the equating—or better, the *calibration*—of test scores, one that permits test forms to reflect their characteristics on the scale. For this purpose a convenient analogy may be found in the measurement of degrees of heat. On the one hand, there is the scale of temperature as one that extends from about −460° Fahrenheit (−273°C.) upwards; on the other hand, there is a specific measuring instrument—thermometer—designed to measure degrees of heat in a certain region on the scale of temperature. Each type of thermometer is explicitly constructed for a separate and different purpose. There is the thermometer that is designed to measure the temperature in the householder's bedroom, a thermometer which is constructed and calibrated to yield reasonably accurate measurements of temperature ranging from, say, 40° Fahrenheit to 100° Fahrenheit; measurement beyond those limits is seldom necessary. There is also the thermometer that is constructed and calibrated to yield highly accurate measurements of body temperature, this over the relatively narrow range from about 94° Fahrenheit to 108° Fahrenheit. And there is the thermometer that is constructed and calibrated to yield measurement in the higher ranges of temperature for the purpose of measuring the heat of molten steel. Thus, each thermometer measures appropriately for its purpose but in a different range on the temperature scale.

The parallel between the scale of temperature and the scale of the ability measured by a system of tests is not an unreasonable one. Ideally this situation can be described by imagining that a long and reliable test of the ability under consideration has been constructed and it has been scaled in any one of the ways that have been discussed above. This test and the scale that is defined for it become the basic reference for the entire system of forms to follow. Later forms, when they are introduced, will be calibrated to that reference form and, consequently, to the scale. Thus, as in figure 2, the result of calibrating Form A to the reference scale is that the 60-item test, Form A, yields a range of scaled scores running from about 40 to 160. (The raw score scales of the five forms in figure 2 are drawn to exhibit a linear relationship with the scale that is defined for the reference form. This need not be the case, of course. The linear relationship is used here for the sake of simplicity in the illustration.) The result of calibrating Form B (also 60 items) to the scale is that that form yields a range of scaled scores from about 50 to 170. From the comparison of these two ranges it would appear that Form B is generally a harder test than Form A. Given a group of individuals whose mean ability would best be represented by a score of, say, 120 on the reference scale, their mean *raw* score on Form A would be about 40, but their mean raw score on Form B would be lower, only

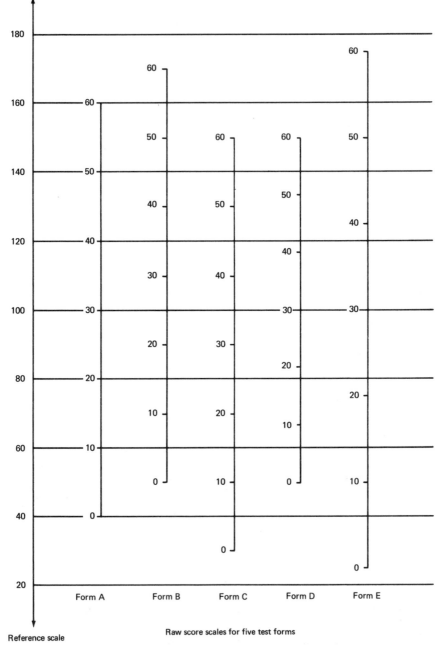

Reference scale

Raw score scales for five test forms

Fig. 2. Relation between the raw score scales of five test forms
and scores on the reference scale

about 35. Another way of saying this is to observe that the mean item difficulty for such a group on these 60-item tests would be .67 for Form A and .58 for Form B. It also is observed that both 60-item forms appear to measure the same range of scaled scores, about 120 points, and are therefore about equally precise. Form C, on the other hand, appears to be a very easy form; the mean p value for the group of individuals with mean ability score of 120 would be as high as .75. Of these three forms, Form C has the lowest ceiling and would therefore be expected to provide the poorest differentiation among the higher ability individuals. It also has the lowest floor and therefore may be expected to provide the best differentiation among lower ability individuals. Form D appears to measure the narrowest range of talent; it gives poor discrimination at both the lower and the higher levels of ability. However, within the limits of its range it appears to measure more accurately than do the other forms, an observation that may be verified from an examination of the standard deviation of raw scores on this form for some appropriate group of examinees in comparison with the standard deviation of raw scores on other forms for the same group of examinees. This observation will be discussed in more detail below. However, for the moment it may suffice to say that one is dealing with a test in which the same number (60) of items are operating within a narrow range of scores (from about 50 to about 150 on the scale, about 100 points) and which is, therefore, making finer discriminations within the scale than Form E, for example, which operates within a range of about 150 points on the scale. Similar kinds of judgments regarding the relative difficulties of the various forms in the system, the ranges of talent over which they differentiate among individuals, and the degree to which they differentiate accurately can be made from a study of the results of the calibration.

Although the model just described for the calibration of test forms provides a convenient and familiar backdrop for consideration of the issues, it is a model that obviously assumes more than is warranted by the facts. It implies, for example, that calibration need not involve an equation of any higher order than the linear equation—that no moments beyond the second need be considered in calibrating one form to another. This is not necessarily so, of course. The restriction to a linear equation has no fundamental theoretical justification and is probably little more than a reflection of the early state of the art. Secondly, the model obviously implies far greater precision in the methods of calibration and also in the tests themselves than is the case. The precision of the techniques of educational measurement rarely, if ever, warrants the degree of precision implied by the results shown in figure 2.

Throughout the course of this description of the calibration model, the analogy has been drawn, and will continue to be drawn, between the calibration of test scores and the calibration of physical measuring instruments. It needs little elaboration to make the point that, while this analogy is a useful one, it is, like all analogies, limited and incomplete, grossly so here because of the vast difference in precision between the two kinds of measurements. In the case of the temperature scale, for example, the distinction between equating and calibration is essentially nonexistent. The result of a measurement of temperature will be the same, whatever thermometer is used to make that measurement—so long as it is appropriately constructed and calibrated to yield that result. This is not so in educational measurement. Two tests that are designed to discriminate over different but overlapping ranges of ability and calibrated accordingly will not necessarily, even in the long run, yield the same score for an individual of given ability. If properly *equated,* however, they *will* yield the same score. Thus, the thermometer analogy may be useful here *for the very reason* that it is incomplete and for the reason that it points to the need for the two separate models in the consideration of score conversions.

The model just described also permits one to consider the calibration of test forms that are not only unequally difficult but unequally reliable as well. Procedures for dealing with the problem of unequal reliabilities will be outlined later on in this chapter. However, the model bears on the distinction between equating and calibration and is relevant here. If one insists on the interchangeability of scores on alternate forms as a prerequisite for the equating model, then there is some serious question about the appropriateness of attempting to equate unequally reliable tests, however the equating is accomplished. Lord[16] has pointed out that there is no single transformation of units for unequally reliable tests that will render the scores interchangeable, since no such transformation will make the true score distributions (standard deviation equaling $s_1\sqrt{r_{11}}$) equal *and at the same time* make the distributions of estimated true scores (standard deviation equaling $s_1 r_{11}$) equal. This condition is necessary for scores to be considered equivalent and interchangeable. The author is inclined to agree and would add the point that scores earned on two tests that are unequally reliable are *for that very reason* not interchangeable; nor is there any equating procedure or transformation of units possible that will make the scores earned on those tests equally reliable and therefore interchangeable. If, however, one considers the calibration model, for which the criterion of interchangeability throughout the range of scores is not intended to apply, then it may be quite reasonable to think of tests of different reliability as being

[16]Personal communication, February 1967.

"referred" to the same psychological scale, in the same sense that thermometers of different precision may be referred to the same scale of temperature. Here too, it is noted, the thermometers are not interchangeable for the very reason that they are not equally precise.

Thus it is found that the five forms of the 60-item test illustrated in figure 2, while all equally long in terms of numbers of items, do not all discriminate over the same number of scale units. That this is evidence of their different reliabilities is not only intuitively reasonable but is observed, as it will be below, when their standard errors of measurement, expressed in terms of the reference scale, are shown to be different and in a predictable way.

There are thus two models of scale adjustment to account for differences in difficulty and range of measured ability. One is the linear, or z-score, model of score *calibration,* a way by which the level and range of ability over which the test is intended to discriminate are reflected in the scores on the reference scale. The other is the curvilinear or equipercentile model (and method) of *equating,* to which the linear method is sometimes a good approximation. Indeed, the linear method is equivalent to the equipercentile method when the shapes of the distributions are the same, that is when, except for the first two, all standardized moments of the distributions of raw scores on the two tests for any given group of examinees are the same. When the raw scores for each of two unequally difficult tests are converted by both methods to a scale that is separate and different from each of the two original raw score scales, it becomes clear that the two models are necessarily different, indeed antithetical. Within the error of the system the linear method reflects its characteristics in the scaled scores it produces; and if the tests differ in difficulty, it will yield scaled scores for one form that cannot be achieved by examinees who take the other form. The equipercentile method, on the other hand, adjusts for these differences, thus ensuring that, within the error of equating, the scaled score for an individual will be the same *regardless* of the characteristics of the form he took.

Methods for Equating Test Forms

In the last 15 or 20 years, with the appearance of new testing programs and offerings, and with the growth and further development of old ones, all requiring the administration of interchangeable test forms, many new designs and methods have been developed and refined for the equating of test scores. These various methods differ in a number of respects. Some require the administration of a single test, others require more than one; some deal with analytical statistics (means, variances, correlations), others deal with the graphical treatment of percentiles;

finally, some—indeed, most—deal with score data, others with item data. The discussion that follows attempts to make a classification of the various methods. In the case of each method in which score data are used, two procedures will be offered where possible, a linear and analytical procedure and also its curvilinear or equipercentile analog. Also, in each case, the linear method may be taken to be an approximation to the equipercentile method when the distributions are similar. It also may be taken as a method of calibration in its own right, whether the distributions are similar or not.

Design I: Random groups—one test administered to each group

In this method a large group of examinees is selected who are sufficiently heterogeneous to sample adequately all levels of score on both forms (X and Y) of the test. (Since, in this method as in all other methods, it is assumed that Forms X and Y are parallel in function at least, it is not necessary to draw the group from some defined population. It is sufficient to say that the population must be one whose level and range of ability are adequately represented by the general level and range of difficulty of the items on the two forms. If the tests *are* parallel, then the resulting conversion of scores from X to Y should be unique, except for random errors of equating, and not associated with the particular kind of group used in the equating.) The group is divided into two random halves, one half (α) taking Form X, the other half (β) taking Form Y. A simple and effective way to form random halves of the group is to package the test books in alternating sequence and to pass them out to the examinees as they are removed one by one from the top of the package. This procedure will fail to yield randomly equivalent subgroups only when the examinees themselves are seated in a sequence (e.g., boy, girl, boy, girl, etc.) that may be correlated with test score.

A. *Equally reliable tests*

1. *Linear procedure*

Following equation 7, the means and standard deviations—on Form X for Group α and on Form Y for Group β—are calculated. The standard-score deviates (z_{x_α} and z_{y_β}) for the two groups are then set equal,

$$\frac{Y - M_{y_\beta}}{s_{y_\beta}} = \frac{X - M_{x_\alpha}}{s_{x_\alpha}}.$$ [8]

When the terms of equation 8 are rearranged they yield the linear equation,

$$Y = \frac{s_{y_\beta}}{s_{x_\alpha}} X + M_{y_\beta} - \frac{s_{y_\beta}}{s_{x_\alpha}} M_{x_\alpha},$$ [9]

which is of the form, $Y=AX+B$, where A (the slope of the conversion line) $=s_{y_\beta}/s_{x_\alpha}$, and B (the intercept of the conversion line) $=M_{y_\beta}-AM_{x_\alpha}$. This conversion equation, like all score conversions, is symmetrical; unlike regression equations, the same equation may be used for converting scores from the scale of Form X to the scale of Form Y, or from the scale of Y to the scale of X.

If Form Y is an earlier form of the test for which there already exists a conversion to the reference scale, C—let us say, in the form of the equation, $C=A'Y+B'$—then the substitution in it of the equation $Y=AX+B$, will yield a new equation, $C=A''X+B''$, relating raw scores on Form X directly to the scale, where $A''=A'A$ and $B''=A'B+B'$.

The foregoing linear *equating* (preferably, *calibration*) will make it possible to illustrate some of the observations made about figure 2. Say that there are five 60-item forms of a test on which scaled scores are to be reported. Also say that each of the five forms was administered to a random fifth of a large group (a testing plan which represents a simple extension of the random-halves administration just described). Finally, say that there already exists an equation relating Form A, the first of the five forms, to the reference scale: $C=2.0X_a+40$. When projected on the scale, this form yields a minimum scaled score of 40 $[C=(2.0)(0)+40]$, a maximum scaled score of 160 $[C=(2.0)(60)+40]$, and a range of scaled scores of 120, i.e., $160 - 40$.

Now equate Form B to Form A. Using the data from the administration, shown in table 3, and substituting in equation 8, it is found that $(X_a-30)/10=(X_b-25)/10$, or $X_a=X_b+5$. Substituting into the equation relating Form A to the scale, $C=2.0X_a+40$, the equation relating Form B to the scale, $C=2.0X_b+50$ is found. Form B is clearly a more difficult test than Form A, since it yields a mean of only 25 for a group of individuals who are essentially equivalent in ability to a group who earned a mean of 30 on Form A. This greater difficulty of Form B is reflected in the minimum and maximum scaled scores, 50 and 170, which, of course, are determined by the scaled score conversion equation

TABLE 3

Scaled Score Values for Five Forms of a 60-Item Test

Form	Raw Score Statistics		Conversion Equation	Scale Values		Range
	M_x	s_x		Minimum	Maximum	
A	30	10	$C=2.00X_a+40$	40	160	120
B	25	10	$C=2.00X_b+50$	50	170	120
C	35	10	$C=2.00X_c+30$	30	150	120
D	30	12	$C=1.67X_d+50$	50	150	100
E	30	8	$C=2.50X_e+25$	25	175	150

for Form B. The more difficult the form, the higher is the "location" of that form on the reference scale. Similarly, the easier the form, the lower is the "location" of that form on the reference scale, as may be seen by examining the statistics for Form C. Form C has a higher raw score mean than either Form A or Form B, and as a result appears lower on the scale, with a minimum scaled score of 30 and a maximum of 150. However, since the raw score standard deviations for Forms A, B, and C are the same, their ranges of measurement, as reflected on the scale, are also the same. Form D, on the other hand, has a large raw score standard deviation and therefore discriminates over a narrow range on the scale; Form E has a small raw score standard deviation and therefore discriminates over a wide range on the scale. It appears to be intuitively reasonable that difficult forms should appear higher on the scale than easy forms. A raw score of 40 on a generally difficult form *should* represent a higher level of talent than a raw score of 40 on an easier form. Similarly, it is intuitively reasonable that forms with larger raw score standard deviations should encompass a narrower range of scaled scores since large standard deviations of raw scores are characteristic of more reliable tests. It also would be expected that of two equally long forms the form that discriminates over a narrower range of talent would be the more reliable form. This general observation is further confirmed by an examination of the standard errors of measurement for tests that have different standard deviations, say, Forms D and E, as expressed on the reference scale. The raw score standard errors of measurement at score 30 are both about 3.9, as calculated by a formula developed by Lord (1957). However, when the standard errors of measurement are expressed in comparable terms, that is to say, on the reference scale, it turns out that Form D is much more precise than Form E. The scaled score standard error of measurement is about 6.5 (3.9 times 1.67, the slope of the conversion line) for Form D but as much as 9.8 (3.9 times 2.50) for Form E, consistent with what one would expect from the relative sizes of their standard deviations. It is in this way that the linear transformation makes it possible to observe fairly directly the properties of difficulty and discrimination for the various forms.

Like all statistical procedures, equating is, of course, also subject to random error, arising here from the sampling fluctuations of the means and standard deviations of scores on Forms X and Y. The standard error of equating (Lord, 1950) is described as the standard deviation of converted scores on the scale of Y, corresponding to a fixed value of X, in which each converted Y score is taken from a conversion line that results from an independent sampling of Groups α and β from a basic group that is normally distributed in both X and Y. The standard error of equating by the method just described is given, approximately, in the equation:

$$SE^2_{y*} = \frac{2s^2_y}{N_t}(z^2_x + 2),$$ [10]

where SE^2_{y*} = the variance error of equated Y scores,
$N_t = N_\alpha + N_\beta$, and
$z_x = (X - M_x)/s_x$.

From equation 10 it can be seen that the variance error of equating by equation 9 is 1.5 times as large at 1 standard deviation away from the mean of X as it is at the mean, 3 times as large at 2 standard deviations from the mean, and more than 4 times as large at 2.5 standard deviations from the mean.

2. *Curvilinear analog*

Two distributions are formed, one on Form X for Group α and another on Form Y for Group β. Mid-percentile ranks, or relative cumulative frequencies (i.e., percentage of cases falling below each interval) if that is more convenient, are then computed for each distribution, as in table 4, and plotted and smoothed, as in figure 3. The general principles of hand smoothing have been described in the section on scaling, in which it was pointed out that the experience and judgment of the person working with the data will determine the degree to which irregularities in the data are defined as such and smoothed out. Indeed, it is this subjectivity, necessarily part of the hand smoothing process in equipercentile equating, that has helped to cause some test constructors to avoid it and to prefer analytic linear methods of equating instead.

Distributions also may be smoothed analytically before they are plotted. Two such procedures were mentioned in this chapter in connection with normalized scales and also in the section of this chapter on norms. One is a rolling weighted average method developed by Cureton and Tukey (1951). Another method, which is at present appropriate only to rights-scored tests, is derived from the negative hypergeometric distribution (Keats & Lord, 1962).

Difficulties in smoothing by hand are frequently encountered near the ends of the distributions where data are relatively scant. Sometimes data run out before the minimum and maximum scores on the test are reached, with the result that the ogives (and, later in the equating process, the conversion curve itself) have to be extrapolated without the benefit of supporting data. Obviously, such a procedure can lead to intolerably large errors. It is for this reason, to give adequate representation in data to all score levels on the tests, that it is desirable to use

TABLE 4

Distributions of Raw Scores on Two Forms of the STEP Social Studies Test

RAW SCORES	FORM 1a Frequency Grade 12	Grade 13	Combined Frequency	Cumulative Frequency	Percentage Below	FORM 2a Frequency Grade 12	Grade 13	Combined Frequency	Cumulative Frequency	Percentage Below
68–69							2	2	677	99.7
66–67							2	2	675	99.4
64–65							6	6	673	98.5
62–63	1	2	3	689	99.6	2	5	7	667	97.5
60–61	0	3	3	686	99.1	3	9	12	660	95.7
58–59	0	5	5	683	98.4	4	21	25	648	92.0
56–57	0	6	6	678	97.5	4	17	21	623	88.9
54–55	4	7	11	672	95.9	6	28	34	602	83.9
52–53	2	14	16	661	93.6	15	14	29	568	79.6
50–51	4	14	18	645	91.0	16	28	44	539	73.1
48–49	5	16	21	627	88.0	20	26	46	495	66.3
46–47	10	24	34	606	83.0	23	30	53	449	58.5
44–45	13	25	38	572	77.5	23	23	46	396	51.7
42–43	11	24	35	534	72.4	28	18	46	350	44.9
40–41	10	18	28	499	68.4	19	24	43	304	38.6
38–39	18	19	37	471	63.0	25	19	44	261	32.1
36–37	17	23	40	434	57.2	31	16	47	217	25.1
34–35	27	18	45	394	50.7	23	13	36	170	19.8
32–33	21	21	42	349	44.6	22	12	34	134	14.8
30–31	26	31	57	307	36.3	16	8	24	100	11.2
28–29	29	26	55	250	28.3	15	5	20	76	8.3
26–27	32	15	47	195	21.5	12	6	18	56	5.6
24–25	24	14	38	148	16.0	7	4	11	38	4.0
22–23	27	9	36	110	10.7	7	4	11	27	2.4
20–21	23	11	34	74	5.8	3	3	6	16	1.5
18–19	14	3	17	40	3.3	4	1	5	10	0.7
16–17	8	4	12	23	1.6	2	1	3	5	0.3
14–15	6	1	7	11	0.6	2		2	2	
12–13	3	0	3	4	0.1					
10–11		1	1	1						

relatively heterogeneous groups for equating, sampling the cases particularly heavily at the ends of the raw score range.

When the ogives for both Forms X and Y have been plotted and smoothed, corresponding percentiles are read from each smoothed ogive, recorded as in table 5, and plotted, one against the other, on arithmetic graph paper, as in figure 4. Generally, 30 points or so are adequate to describe the relationship between the two tests. The curve connecting these points is similarly smoothed and also extrapolated to the endpoints on the test in order to cover the full range of possible scores. The resulting smoothed curve is used to record the conversion from Form X to Form Y and vice versa (table 6). Additional smoothing can be done in the recorded values by computing differences between the successive

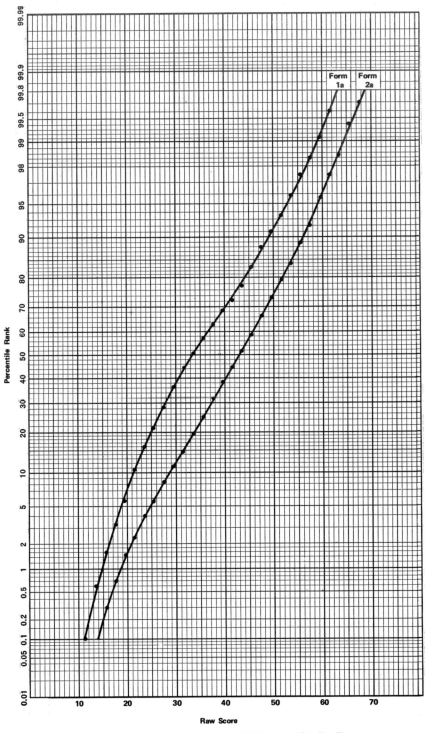

FIG. 3. Ogives for two forms of the STEP Social Studies Test
(plotted on arithmetic probability paper)

TABLE 5

Equipercentile Points on Two Forms of the STEP Social Studies Test

PERCENTILE RANK	RAW SCORE ON FORM 1a	2a	PERCENTILE RANK	RAW SCORE ON FORM 1a	2a
0.2	12.0	15.0	54	34.6	44.0
0.3	12.7	15.7	62	37.2	46.1
0.7	14.0	17.6	70	40.1	48.6
1.2	15.1	19.0	77	42.9	50.6
2	16.1	20.9	83	45.4	53.0
3	17.1	22.3	88	48.0	55.0
5	18.8	24.8	92	50.2	57.0
8	20.4	27.3	95	53.0	59.0
12	22.1	30.0	97	55.1	61.0
17	24.0	32.4	98	56.9	62.1
23	25.9	35.0	98.8	58.6	64.0
30	27.9	37.2	99.3	60.0	65.4
38	30.0	39.5	99.7	62.1	67.5
46	32.3	42.0	99.8	63.1	68.9
50	33.3	43.0			

TABLE 6

Equivalent Raw Scores on Two Forms of the STEP Social Studies Test

FORM 2a	FORM 1a	FORM 2a	FORM 1a	FORM 2a	FORM 1a	FORM 2a	FORM 1a
0	2.5	18	14.3	36	26.8	54	46.7
1	3.1	19	15.0	37	27.7	55	47.9
2	3.8	20	15.6	38	28.6	56	49.1
3	4.4	21	16.3	39	29.5	57	50.3
4	5.0	22	16.9	40	30.4	58	51.5
5	5.7	23	17.6	41	31.3	59	52.7
6	6.4	24	18.2	42	32.3	60	53.9
7	7.0	25	18.9	43	33.3	61	55.1
8	7.7	26	19.5	44	34.4	62	56.3
9	8.4	27	20.2	45	35.6	63	57.4
10	9.1	28	20.8	46	36.8	64	58.5
11	9.7	29	21.5	47	38.0	65	59.5
12	10.4	30	22.2	48	39.3	66	60.5
13	11.0	31	23.0	49	40.6	67	61.5
14	11.7	32	23.7	50	41.8	68	62.5
15	12.3	33	24.5	51	43.0	69	63.4
16	13.0	34	25.2	52	44.3	70	64.2
17	13.6	35	26.0	53	45.5		

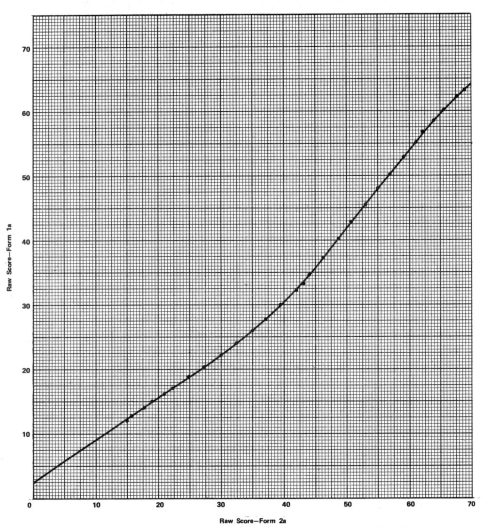

FIG. 4. Equivalent raw scores on two forms of the STEP Social Studies Test, derived by equipercentile equating

values and adjusting them to yield a smooth progression of numbers. The values in table 6 are ordinarily rounded and reported in the test manuals to the nearest whole numbers.

B. *Unequally reliable tests (linear calibration)*

It has already been pointed out that when the two forms are not interchangeable—for example when their reliabilities are unequal—their scores cannot be "equated" in any meaningful way. Therefore, there will be no attempt made here to discuss the "equating" of unequally reliable tests (i.e., by equipercentile methods). However, the calibration of unequally reliable tests *can* be discussed, because in that model there is no issue of interchangeability. Each test form discriminates within a region of the ability continuum and at a level of precision peculiar to the test form itself. For forms known to differ significantly in reliability it is not only appropriate but preferable that the calibration involve true scores rather than observed scores, as in the equation:

$$\frac{Y - M_{y_\beta}}{s_{\tilde{y}_\beta}} = \frac{X - M_{x_\alpha}}{s_{\tilde{x}_\alpha}},$$

where $s_{\tilde{x}} = s_x \sqrt{r_{xx}}$ and $s_{\tilde{y}} = s_y \sqrt{r_{yy}}$. The equation for converting scores from the scale of Form X to the scale of Form Y becomes:

$$Y = \frac{s_{\tilde{y}_\beta}}{s_{\tilde{x}_\alpha}} X + M_{y_\beta} - \frac{s_{\tilde{y}_\beta}}{s_{\tilde{x}_\alpha}} M_{x_\alpha},$$

also of the form $Y = AX + B$, where $A = s_{\tilde{y}_\beta} / s_{\tilde{x}_\alpha}$ and $B = M_{y_\beta} - AM_{x_\alpha}$.

Design II: Random groups—both tests administered to each group, counterbalanced

As in design I a large group of individuals is selected and divided into two random halves, one half (α) taking Form X followed by Form Y, the other half (β) taking Form Y followed by Form X. In order to guard against errors in administration it is advisable, especially when Forms X and Y are administered in one extended testing session (as is desirable if communication among examinees is to be controlled), to bind the pairs of test books together, half with Form X on top and half with Form Y on top. The booklet sets would then be packaged in alternating sequence (XY, YX, XY, YX, etc.) and distributed in that order to the examinees.

A. *Equally reliable tests*

    1. *Linear procedure*

In this method, given by Lord (1950), it is assumed that the practice effect on Form Y as a result of having taken Form X first and the practice effect on Form X as a result of having taken Form Y first are proportional to the standard deviations of the two tests: $K_x/s_x = K_y/s_y = H$. Also, the best estimate of H is taken to be the average of the differences between the means on Form X and the means on Form Y when each is expressed in standard deviation units:

$$H = \frac{1}{2} \left(\frac{M_{x_\beta} - M_{x_\alpha}}{s_x} + \frac{M_{y_\alpha} - M_{y_\beta}}{s_y} \right).$$

It is recalled that the prototype of the equation for the linear equating of test scores is given by equation 7, $(Y-M_y)/s_y=(X-M_x)/s_x$. The formulas to use for obtaining the values to be substituted in equation 7 are given as follows:

$$M_x = \tfrac{1}{2}(M_{x_\alpha} + M_{x_\beta} - K_x), \qquad\qquad [11]$$
$$M_y = \tfrac{1}{2}(M_{y_\alpha} + M_{y_\beta} - K_y), \qquad\qquad [12]$$
$$s_x^2 = \tfrac{1}{2}(s_{x_\alpha}^2 + s_{x_\beta}^2), \qquad\qquad [13]$$

and

$$s_y^2 = \tfrac{1}{2}(s_{y_\alpha}^2 + s_{y_\beta}^2). \qquad\qquad [14]$$

When equations 11 to 14 are substituted in equation 7, a linear equation of the form $Y=AX+B$ is found, where

$$A = \sqrt{\frac{s_{y_\alpha}^2 + s_{y_\beta}^2}{s_{x_\alpha}^2 + s_{x_\beta}^2}},$$

and

$$B = \frac{1}{2}(M_{y_\alpha} + M_{y_\beta}) - \frac{A}{2}(M_{x_\alpha} + M_{x_\beta}).$$

If it may be assumed that the bivariate surface of X versus Y is normal for the population of which the two half-groups are samples, and if it may also be assumed that the standard deviations for each form and the correlation between forms are the same in the population, then the variance error of scores converted to the scale of Y (Lord, 1950) is found to be approximately:

$$SE_{y*}^2 = s_y^2(1 - r_{xy})\frac{z_x^2(1 + r_{xy}) + 2}{N_t}, \qquad\qquad [15]$$

in which z_x is defined as before: $z_x=(X-M_x)/s_x$. That the counterbalanced method of equating is highly precise may be observed by comparing its variance error, given in equation 15, with the variance error in equation 10 for the linear equating method in design I. For two forms that correlate .80, for example, the variance error of converted Y scores at $z_x=0$ is one-tenth the size of the error of design I; that is to say, one would need *10 times* the number of cases for equating by design I in order to achieve the precision provided by design II.

A variant of this procedure is to combine the data on Form X of the two half-groups, combine the data on Form Y for the two half-groups, and equate by the method described in design I.

2. Curvilinear analog

The curvilinear analog of the counter-balanced method is one that corresponds to the procedure described briefly in the preceding paragraph, in which data on Form X and also on Form Y are combined for the two half-groups, and the equipercentile procedure described in design I is applied.

B. *Unequally reliable tests (linear calibration)*

When Forms X and Y are unequally reliable, the average within-group variance should be calculated not on the basis of observed scores, as shown in equations 13 and 14, but on the basis of true scores. The appropriate values, corresponding to those in equations 13 and 14, are given in equations 16 and 17:

$$s_{\tilde{x}}^2 = \tfrac{1}{2} (s_{x_\alpha}^2 r_{xx_\alpha} + s_{x_\beta}^2 r_{xx_\beta}),$$ [16]

and

$$s_{\tilde{y}}^2 = \tfrac{1}{2} (s_{y_\alpha}^2 r_{yy_\alpha} + s_{y_\beta}^2 r_{yy_\beta}).$$ [17]

In addition to its greater stability—which is to be expected in view of the fact that it makes use of so much more data than the methods of design I—design II enjoys the additional advantage that it makes it possible to obtain two independent determinations of the parallel-forms reliability coefficient. On the other hand, it does require twice as much administration time as does design I and therefore imposes an administrative burden on participating schools, which occasionally makes it difficult to obtain subjects. Another disadvantage of the method is that it is sensitive to clerical errors. Since the method does depend on the separation of examinees taking the tests in the two orders, special pains must be taken that the candidates do take the tests in the order designated for them and that the answer sheets be accurately identified not only as to the form of the test but also as to its ordinal position in the administration.

Design III: Random groups—one test administered to each group, common equating test administered to both groups

A. *Equally reliable tests (linear calibration)*

The methods described under designs I and II are appropriate only in those situations which permit the assignment of examinees to *random groups*. (This is particularly true of design I, which is likely to be much more sensitive than design II to the demand for random assignment.) The significance of this point may become clearer if the purpose of equating is reconsidered: Any raw score, or any statistic that is taken over raw scores, is a function of *both* the ability (abilities) of the individual(s) *and* the characteristics of the test. In order to compare the performances of individuals (or groups) who have taken different tests, it is necessary to make prior adjustments in the test scores—i.e., to equate the tests—so that differences in the scores (or in the statistics) will insofar as possible be solely the result of differences in the individuals (or groups). The adjustment that is sought in the test scores must therefore be a function *only* of the differences in the tests, uncontaminated by the characteristics of the groups that were originally used to determine the adjustment. (To draw on the temperature-thermometer analogy again: the equation, $F=1.8C+32$, is useful because it is independent of the method used to derive it and *also* independent of the substances used in the derivation—in addition to the fact that it is universally applicable.) Reference to equations 8 and 9 makes it clear that if Groups α and β are not drawn at random from the same population, differences between them can represent a very significant factor in altering the A and B values and introducing major sources of bias into the equation. However, even where the groups *are* chosen at random, there will inevitably be small differences between them which, if disregarded, will appear in the conversion equation as precisely the kind of bias that has just been discussed, a persistent and ineradicable source of error that will affect all individual and group comparisons that depend on it. Clearly, greater control over the equivalence of the groups used in the equating cannot help but enhance the precision of the equating.

In order to effect this control, the methods of equating and calibration to be described in this section and all others to follow make use of a test score, U, based on a set of items in addition to (or common to) those represented by Forms X and Y, that is used to adjust for the differences that may be found to exist between Groups α and β. In the administration of the tests, Form U is given with Form X to Group α. The identical Form U is also given with Form Y to Group β. Equations appropriate to a random administration of X and Y, with U administered to all examinees, have been developed by Lord (1955a) in a derivation in which he makes maximum likelihood estimates of the population means and variances on Forms X and Y. These equations are:

$$\hat{\mu}_x = M_{x_\alpha} + b_{xu_\alpha}(\hat{\mu}_u - M_{u_\alpha}), \qquad [18]$$

$$\hat{\mu}_y = M_{y_\beta} + b_{yu_\beta}(\hat{\mu}_u - M_{u_\beta}), \qquad [19]$$

$$\hat{\sigma}_x^2 = s_{x_\alpha}^2 + b_{xu_\alpha}^2(\hat{\sigma}_u^2 - s_{u_\alpha}^2), \qquad [20]$$

$$\hat{\sigma}_y^2 = s_{y_\beta}^2 + b_{yu_\beta}^2(\hat{\sigma}_u^2 - s_{u_\beta}^2), \qquad [21]$$

where $\hat{\mu}_u = M_{u_t}$ and $\hat{\sigma}_u^2 = s_{u_t}^2$, and $t = \alpha + \beta$. These estimates are applied as before to equation 7, to form the conversion equation, $Y = AX + B$, where $A = \hat{\sigma}_y/\hat{\sigma}_x$ and $B = \hat{\mu}_y - A\hat{\mu}_x$.

The error variance for this method of equating is given by Lord (1950) as:

$$\mathrm{SE}_{y^*}^2 = 2\hat{\sigma}_y^2\,(1 - \hat{r}^2)\,\frac{(1 + \hat{r}^2)z_x^2 + 2}{N_t}, \qquad [22]$$

approximately, in which it is assumed that

$$\hat{r} = \frac{b_{xu_\alpha}\hat{\sigma}_u}{\hat{\sigma}_x} = \frac{b_{yu_\beta}\hat{\sigma}_u}{\hat{\sigma}_y}.$$

From this it is seen that when $\hat{r} = 0$, this error variance is the same as that for the linear method of design I. When $\hat{r} = .70$, it is one-half as large at the mean ($z_x = 0$) as that for design I. When $\hat{r} = .87$ it is one-fourth as large at the mean as that for design I.

It may be helpful to examine equations 18 to 21 in a little detail. If Groups α and β are identical in their mean performance on Form U, then the values of the parenthetical terms in equations 18 and 19 are found to be zero. That is to say, group adjustments are unnecessary, and the best population estimates of mean scores on Forms X and Y are the means that were actually observed for Groups α and β. Similar kinds of considerations, of course, apply to equations 20 and 21.

It is also noted in these equations that no restrictions are placed on the nature of Form U. It is clear, however, that the usefulness of Form U for equating depends on the extent to which it is correlated with the tests being equated. If, for example, $r_{xu} = 0$ (and, presumably, $r_{yu} = 0$, since X and Y are parallel forms), this would indicate that observations made on Form U are irrelevant to the psychological functions measured by Form X or Form Y and are therefore not useful in making adjustments in these measures. This might be true if Forms X and Y were measures of mathematical aptitude for college freshmen and Form U, to take an extreme example, were a measure of height. Obviously, observations made on a variable like height are useless in determining the extent of the adjustments that should be made in a variable like mathematical aptitude. In a manner of speaking, then, the correlation, r_{xu}, which is part of the regression coefficient, b_{xu}, and expresses the degree of relevance that Form U bears to Form X, determines the extent to which the amount of the difference in the parenthetical term may be utilized in making the adjustments for the differences in the groups. The ratio, s_x/s_u, which is the other part of the regression coefficient, may be regarded as a scaling factor used to convert the parenthetical expression from the scale of Form U to the scale of Form X.

The great advantage of this method of equating is its flexibility and adaptability to varying conditions. Form U may be administered in addition to and separate from Form X and/or Form Y. The expression *and/or* is to be noted especially. There is no need for Form U to play precisely the same role in both Forms X and Y. It may be an integral part of Form X, for example, but entirely separate from Form Y. It may be a separately timed section of Forms X and Y. Indeed—and this characteristic endows it with a wide range of administrative power—it may be included within Forms X and/or Y as a set of discrete items interspersed throughout the tests but capable of yielding a total score. In any case, the fundamental restriction is that, however it is used, Form U must represent *the same kind of task* to Group α as it does to Group β. For example, it must be equally subject to contextual and ordinal effects when taken by the two groups; it must be equally subject to the effects of speededness; and it must be equally subject to the effects of motivation, practice, boredom, or fatigue. Within these obvious, commonsense restrictions, the degrees of flexibility indicated above are quite real. Nevertheless, there are certain practices that are recommended: The equating test (or anchor test, or link test, or common test, as it is variously called), Form U, should be long enough and reliable enough to yield data that can be used effectively for making the fine adjustments for differences between the groups that are required. A recommended rule of thumb is that it consist of no fewer than 20 items or no fewer than 20 percent of the number of items in each of Forms X and Y, whichever number of items is larger. It also has been considered advisable, when Form U is defined as a score based on a set of items interspersed through the operational tests, X and Y, to avoid taking such items from the latter part of the test where the effects of speededness are likely to be pronounced.

The same general principle, that Form U represent the same psychological task to both groups, should be adhered to when it is a separately timed test. For example, it either follows the administration of both X and Y or it precedes them both; it is equally affected by practice (or boredom or fatigue) on X and Y; and it does not repeat any items that already appear in X and Y.

The method of equating described here has other dimensions of flexibility. For example, it allows an economical use of its data for the equating of three or more forms as well as two forms. Say there are three parallel forms to equate: X, Y, and Z. These are administered to groups α, β, and γ, respectively, and the performance (mean and variance) for the combined group $(\alpha+\beta+\gamma)$ is estimated using the same assumptions in the case of the three forms as were made in the equating of two forms. Once these estimates are available they can be entered into the fundamental conversion equation, equation 7, to derive a conversion relating any two of the tests in question.

The method permits other variations. The equating test, Form U, need not be treated as though it were a single variable. It may indeed yield not only one, but two, three, four, or as many scores as are required for making the adjustments between groups. Say that Forms X and Y are alternate forms of a test consisting of *both* verbal and mathematical items. In order to make adjustments for the differences between the groups of individuals taking those forms it would be desirable to use an equating test, Form U, that similarly contains both verbal and mathematical items. The scores on these two kinds of items may be combined to yield a total score, U, and applied as has been described above; on the other hand, they may be *kept separate,* as scores V and M, and used in *multiple combination.* The equations used for estimating the mean and variance for the combined group t on Forms X and Y with the use of a multiple predictor are extensions of equations 18 to 21:

$$\hat{\mu}_x = M_{x_\alpha} + b_{xv \cdot m_\alpha}(\hat{\mu}_v - M_{v_\alpha}) + b_{xm \cdot v_\alpha}(\hat{\mu}_m - M_{m_\alpha}), \qquad [23]$$

$$\hat{\mu}_y = M_{y_\beta} + b_{yv \cdot m_\beta}(\hat{\mu}_v - M_{v_\beta}) + b_{ym \cdot v_\beta}(\hat{\mu}_m - M_{m_\beta}), \qquad [24]$$

$$\hat{\sigma}_x^2 = s_{x_\alpha}^2 + b_{xv \cdot m_\alpha}^2(\hat{\sigma}_v^2 - s_{v_\alpha}^2) + b_{xm \cdot v_\alpha}^2(\hat{\sigma}_m^2 - s_{m_\alpha}^2)$$
$$+ 2b_{xv \cdot m_\alpha}b_{xm \cdot v_\alpha}(\hat{\sigma}_{vm} - s_{vm_\alpha}), \qquad [25]$$

$$\hat{\sigma}_y^2 = s_{y_\beta}^2 + b_{yv \cdot m_\beta}^2(\hat{\sigma}_v^2 - s_v^2) + b_{ym \cdot v_\beta}^2(\hat{\sigma}_{m_\beta}^2 - s_{m_\beta}^2)$$
$$+ 2b_{yv \cdot m_\beta}b_{ym \cdot v_\beta}(\hat{\sigma}_{vm} - s_{vm_\beta}), \qquad [26]$$

where $b_{xv \cdot m_\alpha}$, for example, is the raw-score regression weight for predicting X from V, with M held constant, and $s_{vm_\alpha} = r_{vm_\alpha}s_{v_\alpha}s_{m_\alpha}$. Also, consistent with the notation used in equations 18 to 21, $\hat{\mu}_v = M_{v_t}$, $\hat{\mu}_m = M_{m_t}$, $\hat{\sigma}_v^2 = s_{v_t}^2$, $\hat{\sigma}_m^2 = s_{m_t}^2$, and $\hat{\sigma}_{vm} = s_{vm_t}$. That is to say, the estimates of the population parameters for the common variables, V and M, are taken directly from the corresponding observed statistics for the combined group, $t(t = \alpha + \beta)$.

There is still another variation possible. The equating test, Form U, that is administered to Group α need not be precisely the same test as the Form U administered to Group β. It may be a *quasi-common* test. That is to say, it may actually be *two different forms* of the same test (say U and W), so long as they are both expressed in the same units—that is, so long as the W scores have been converted to the scale of U, or vice versa, or both converted to some other single scale. Any of these variations is possible, the only requirement being that scores on the two forms must be directly and universally comparable. It is understood, of course, that this variation may be introduced not only when the equating test represents a single predictor, but also when it represents multiple predictors, as in equations 23 to 26. Under these circumstances, the two V forms must be expressed on the same scale, as must the two M forms. V and M, however, need not be expressed on similar-appearing scales.

B. *Unequally reliable tests (linear calibration)*

Levine (1955) has shown that, for a random-groups administration, when Forms X and Y are unequally reliable, it is appropriate to base the conversion on *true,* rather than observed, scores. Under this set of conditions, and when Form U is separate and exclusive of X and Y, the slope and intercept of the conversion equation, $Y = AX + B$, are found to be: $A = b_{yu_\beta} / b_{xu_\alpha}$, and $B = \hat{\mu}_y - A\hat{\mu}_x$, where b_{xu_α} and b_{yu_β} are the usual regression coefficients, as observed in Groups α and β, respectively, for predicting X from U and Y from U, and where $\hat{\mu}_x$ and $\hat{\mu}_y$ are calculated as in equations 18 and 19. The additional assumption required in Levine's derivation is that Form U be parallel in function to both Forms X and Y.

When Form U is an included part of X and Y, $A = (b_{xu_\alpha} \hat{\sigma}_y^2) / (b_{yu_\beta} \hat{\sigma}_x^2)$ and $B = \hat{\mu}_y - A\hat{\mu}_x$. The values of $\hat{\mu}_x$, $\hat{\mu}_y$, $\hat{\sigma}_x^2$, and $\hat{\sigma}_y^2$ are calculated as in equations 18 to 21 respectively.

Design IV: Nonrandom groups—one test to each group, common equating test administered to both groups

A. *Basic linear method for groups not widely different in ability*

The methods described under designs I, II, and III are appropriate in situations which permit the assignment of examinees to random groups. However, there are frequently situations, as in the operation of a highly secure testing program, where it is considered inadvisable to introduce new forms prior to their first operational use, even in an experimental equating administration, and where the demands of the program do not permit the presentation of more than one form at an operational administration of the test. Under these circumstances equating based on the random administration of test forms is not possible. The methods of all three of the foregoing designs are ruled out, and the data used for equating have to be drawn from the operational administrations themselves, where little control, if any, can be exercised over the choice of equating samples. If, for example, a new form of a test is introduced at, say, the regular September administration in a testing program and it is desired to equate that form to an older form, even one given at a previous

September administration where the examinees are similar to these in many respects, there would still be no assurance that the groups taking the two forms were drawn from the same population. Therefore, even when care has been taken, as it was in the present example, to choose the α and β groups in such a way as to minimize their differences, some means must be found to observe the differences that do exist between the two groups and to make adjustments for them.

The methods to be described in the present section derive their data from the same design as that previously described in connection with the maximum likelihood method developed by Lord (1955a) and the true-score adaptation of that method by Levine (1955). It may be helpful to recapitulate the essentials of the design: Form X is administered to Group α; Form Y is administered to Group β. Form U, a test which is based on a set of items in addition to (or included among) those represented by Forms X and Y, is administered to both Groups α and β and is used to adjust for differences that may be found to exist between them. Estimates of the mean and variance on both Forms X and Y are made for the combined group, Group t (t representing $\alpha+\beta$), and are applied in equation 7 to yield a linear equation relating raw scores on Form X to raw scores on Form Y. Because the equations that provide these estimates of mean and variance are so basic to the problem of equating, their derivation, attributed to L. R Tucker (Gulliksen, 1950, chap. 19; also Angoff, 1961a), is repeated here. The equations are based on the three principal assumptions of univariate selection theory: that the intercept of X on U is the same for Group t and Group α, i.e.

$$M_{x_t} - b_{xu_t}M_{u_t} = M_{x_\alpha} - b_{xu_\alpha}M_{u_\alpha};$$ [27]

that the regression coefficient of X on U is the same for Group t and Group α, i.e.,

$$b_{xu_t} = b_{xu_\alpha};$$ [28]

and that the variance error of estimate of X from U is the same for Group t and Group α, i.e.,

$$s_{x_t}^2(1 - r_{xu_t}^2) = s_{x_\alpha}^2(1 - r_{xu_\alpha}^2).$$ [29]

Substituting equation 28 in 27 and solving for $\hat{M}_{x_t}$,

$$\hat{M}_{x_t} = M_{x_\alpha} + b_{xu_\alpha}(M_{u_t} - M_{u_\alpha}),$$ [30]

the symbol ($\hat{\ }$) here, as before, designating an estimated value. Substituting, in equation 29, $b_{xu_t}s_{u_t}$ for its equivalent, $r_{xu_t}s_{x_t}$, and also $b_{xu_\alpha}s_{u_\alpha}$ for its equivalent, $r_{xu_\alpha}s_{x_\alpha}$, and solving for $\hat{s}_{x_t}^2$,

$$\hat{s}_{x_t}^2 = s_{x_\alpha}^2 + b_{xu_\alpha}^2 (s_{u_t}^2 - s_{u_\alpha}^2).$$ [31]

Parallel assumptions and development are made for the relationship between Forms Y and U and Groups β and t, resulting in the following two equations which parallel, respectively, equations 30 and 31.

$$\hat{M}_{y_t} = M_{y_\beta} + b_{yu_\beta} (M_{u_t} - M_{u_\beta}),$$ [32]

and

$$\hat{s}_{y_t}^2 = s_{y_\beta}^2 + b_{yu_\beta}^2 (s_{u_t}^2 - s_{u_\beta}^2).$$ [33]

(The symbols $\hat{M}_{x_t}$, $\hat{s}_{x_t}^2$, $\hat{M}_{y_t}$, and $\hat{s}_{y_t}^2$ are used in equations 30 to 33 instead of $\hat{\mu}_x$, $\hat{\sigma}_x^2$, $\hat{\mu}_y$, and $\hat{\sigma}_y^2$, respectively, because here simply an estimate for a combined group is being discussed, not an estimate for a population.) Equations 30 to 33 are then substituted in the prototype equation 7, $(Y-M_y)/s_y = (X-M_x)/s_x$ to yield the conversion equation, $Y=AX+B$, where $A = \hat{s}_{y_t}/\hat{s}_{x_t}$ and $B = \hat{M}_{y_t} - A\hat{M}_{x_t}$.

It is noted that the computational procedures for arriving at the estimates in equations 30 to 33 are precisely the same as for equations 18 to 21 respectively, although the derivations of the two sets of equations are entirely different.

The same kinds of flexibility are appropriate in the present method of equating as in the maximum likelihood method. Form U may be administered in addition to and separate from Form X *and* Form Y, or as part of Form X *and* part of Form Y, or, finally, separate from Form X *but* as part of Form Y. It may be a separately timed section for Forms X and Y, or it may be a set of discrete items interspersed through the two forms but capable of yielding a total score. However, except for the requirement of strict random assignment of Forms X and Y, the basic precautions of administrative design that have been described in connection with the maximum likelihood method are observed here—in sum, that Form U is constructed and administered to represent psychologically the same task to both groups.

The general caution that statistical methods should not be used unless the assumptions that are basic to their derivation can be fulfilled is seldom as clear as it is here. Formulas 30 to 33 are applicable only when it may be assumed that the regression systems for Groups α and β would have been the same had the groups taken precisely the same tests. This is not an unreasonable assumption when the groups are similar in all relevant respects, even if Forms X, Y, and U are not parallel measures. (Lord, 1960, pointed out that, if the groups are very much different in ability, the intercepts of scores on one test on scores on another will differ significantly for the two groups, even if the two tests in question *are* parallel measures.) However, if Form U is *not* parallel to X and Y,[17] then Groups α and β must be drawn at random from the same population. The importance of this requirement can be made clear if one considers as an example the problem of equating two forms (Form X and Form Y) of a test in elementary French grammar at the secondary school level, using performance on a test of verbal aptitude (Form U) to adjust for differences in the groups taking X and Y. Clearly, growth in the function measured by X and Y is much more rapid than growth in the function measured by U. Therefore, if Group α is a group of students who have completed only three months of elementary French while Group β has completed five months of elementary French, one would expect that their scores on the French test would be substantially different even though there were no observable difference in their verbal aptitude. That is to say, under these circumstances, the assumption basic to this equating design, that the regression of scores on X on scores on U (or Y on U) is the same for the two groups, is one that cannot be supported, with the result that the data would be inapplicable to the equating problem.

Like the maximum likelihood method, the method derived from selection theory need not be restricted to the equating of *two* forms of a test but can be used to equate three and more forms. In the administration, each of these forms would be administered to a separate group; but Form U, the equating test, would be given to all groups. Estimates would then be made of the mean and variance on each of the test forms to be equated for the total group taking Form U, in accordance with equations 30 and 31, and carried out as many times as there are forms to be equated. Also, as in the maximum likelihood method, Form U need not be restricted to yielding a single score but may yield a number of scores used in multiple combination in a manner parallel to that described in equations 23 to 26.

Finally, Form U may be a *quasi-common* test. That is to say, it may actually be two different forms of a test, one administered to Group α and the other to Group β. The only restriction is that the two forms be expressed on the same scale, so that appropriate comparisons and adjustments may be made for differences between the two groups in the process of equating the tests.

These variations, it should be pointed out, need not be introduced singly into the basic procedure but may be used in combination. It is entirely possible, for example, to equate four tests simultaneously, using four different forms of Form U (so long as they are all expressed on the

[17]The assumption is still made that Forms X and Y are parallel. This assumption is never relinquished in considering the problems of equating and calibration.

same scale) and, in addition, providing for two separate subscores of each Form U to be used in multiple combination, as in equations 23 to 26.

B. *Curvilinear method for groups not widely different in ability*

An appropriate curvilinear, or equipercentile, analog (suggested by Lord[18] and described by Levine, 1958) to the basic linear equating method described in the preceding section can be derived from the fundamental assumptions stated in equations 27, 28, and 29. If, again, there are two groups of individuals, α and β, one (α) having taken Form X and an equating test U and the other (β) having taken Form Y and the same equating test U, the first step in the equating process is to estimate the frequencies in the distributions of both Form X scores and Form Y scores for the combined group t $(t = \alpha + \beta)$, in a manner precisely the same as was described in the section on norms. This is done by: (*a*) combining the two distributions of Form U scores to form a distribution of Form U scores for Group t; (*b*) working with the scatterplot of U scores versus X scores, multiplying, for each interval of score (i) on Form U, the ratio of frequencies, f_{i_t}/f_{i_α}, by each of the frequencies in the array for score interval U_i. (By varying the size of U_i appropriately it is possible to keep the ratio, f_{i_t}/f_{i_α}, from being excessively large. This is particularly important when the frequencies, f_{i_t} and f_{i_α}, are relatively small.) When this is completed for the arrays for all values of U_i, there will be a new scatterplot of U versus X estimated for Group t. The next steps in the procedure involve: (*c*) making a similar estimate of the frequencies in the scatterplot of U versus Y for Group t; and (*d*) determining the frequencies for each of the scores on Form X (and also on Form Y) simply by adding the frequencies in the cells across the values of U. These frequencies represent the estimated distribution on Form X for the entire Group t, and, correspondingly, the estimated distribution on Form Y for the entire Group t. With these distributions in hand Form X scores can be equated to Form Y scores by the usual equipercentile method. (It should be mentioned that this method, like other "nonrandom-group" methods, is also appropriate under the more restrictive condition in which individuals are assigned to groups at random.)

C. *Linear methods for samples of different ability*

1. *Equally reliable tests*

Levine (1955) has shown that when Groups α and β are widely different in ability the assumptions that are basic to classical selection theory are not appropriate. Instead, other assumptions are made but *under the restriction that Form U is parallel in function to both Forms*

[18]Personal communication, c. 1957.

X and Y: (*a*) that the intercept of the regression line relating true scores on Form X to true scores on Form U (a relationship expressed by a correlation of unity) is the same for Group *t* as for Group *α*:

$$M_{x_t} - \frac{s_{\tilde{x}_t}}{s_{\tilde{u}_t}} M_{u_t} = M_{x_\alpha} - \frac{s_{\tilde{x}_\alpha}}{s_{\tilde{u}_\alpha}} M_{u_\alpha},$$ [34]

where $s_{\tilde{x}} = s_x \sqrt{r_{xx}}$ and $s_{\tilde{u}} = s_u \sqrt{r_{uu}}$; (*b*) that the slope of the line of relationship is the same for Group *t* as for Group *α*:

$$\frac{s_{\tilde{x}_t}}{s_{\tilde{u}_t}} = \frac{s_{\tilde{x}_\alpha}}{s_{\tilde{u}_\alpha}};$$ [35]

and (*c*) that the variance errors of measurement for Form X are the same for Group *t* as for Group *α*:

$$s_{x_t}^2 (1 - r_{xx_t}) = s_{x_\alpha}^2 (1 - r_{xx_\alpha}).$$ [36]

From equations 34, 35, and 36, it can be shown that

$$\hat{M}_{x_t} = M_{x_\alpha} + \frac{s_{\tilde{x}_\alpha}}{s_{\tilde{u}_\alpha}} (M_{u_t} - M_{u_\alpha}),$$ [37]

and that

$$\hat{s}_{x_t}^2 = s_{x_\alpha}^2 + \frac{s_{\tilde{x}_\alpha}^2}{s_{\tilde{u}_\alpha}^2} (s_{u_t}^2 - s_{u_\alpha}^2).$$ [38]

Equations parallel to equations 37 and 38 may be derived by making the same assumptions for the relationship between Form Y and Form U as administered to Groups *t* and *β*, to yield the equations,

$$\hat{M}_{y_t} = M_{y_\beta} + \frac{s_{\tilde{y}_\beta}}{s_{\tilde{u}_\beta}} (M_{u_t} - M_{u_\beta}),$$ [39]

and

$$\hat{s}_{y_t}^2 = s_{y_\beta}^2 + \frac{s_{\tilde{y}_\beta}^2}{s_{\tilde{u}_\beta}^2} (s_{u_t}^2 - s_{u_\beta}^2),$$ [40]

Finally, as before, the conversion equation relating Form X scores to Form Y scores is written $Y = AX + B$, where $A = \hat{s}_{y_t}/\hat{s}_{x_t}$ and $B = \hat{M}_{y_t} - A\hat{M}_{x_t}$. Some simplifications can be introduced into the computation of equations 37 to 40. Angoff (1953) has shown that the data of the equating experiment itself may be used to estimate the ratios of the standard deviations of true scores. In the development of his equations, $s_{\tilde{x}}/s_{\tilde{u}}=n_{xu}$, the ratio of effective test lengths of Form X to Form U. When Form U is included in Form X, the test of parallel function, $n_{xu}=s_x/r_{xu}s_u=1/b_{ux}$; when Form U is separate and exclusive of Form X, then $n_{xu}=(s_x^2+s_{ux})/(s_u^2+s_{ux})$. Similar applications of formulas may, of course, be adopted for the data involving Form Y and Form U.

  2. *Unequally reliable tests*

  When Forms X and Y are unequally reliable, modifications in the equations are required. When Form U is exclusive of X and Y, $Y=AX+B$, where $A=(b_{yu_\beta}r_{uu_\alpha})/(b_{xu_\alpha}r_{uu_\beta})$, and

$$B = M_{y_\beta} - AM_{x_\alpha} + \frac{b_{yu_\beta}}{r_{uu_\beta}}(M_{u_\alpha} - M_{u_\beta}).$$

When Form U is included in X and Y, $A=b_{ux_\alpha}/b_{uy_\beta}$, and $B=M_{y_\beta}-AM_{x_\alpha}+[(M_{u_\alpha}-M_{u_\beta})/b_{uy_\beta}]$.

Design V: Other methods involving score data

  A. *Forms X and Y equated to a common test*

   1. *Linear procedure*

  A method of equating Forms X and Y that is intuitively reasonable is one that, like others just described, also involves the administration of an additional test, U, either following the administration of both X and Y or preceding them both. If X and Y are parallel forms of the same test it is reasonable to assume that each of them has the same practice effect on U when U is administered second, or that U exerts the same practice effect on X and Y, if U is administered first. Form X is equated directly to U; Form Y is equated to U; and scores on X and Y equivalent to the same score on U are themselves taken to be equivalent. Thus, if $X=A_{xu}U+B_{xu}$,[19] where $A_{xu}=s_{x_\alpha}/s_{u_\alpha}$ and $B_{xu}=M_{x_\alpha}-A_{xu}M_{u_\alpha}$, and if $Y=A_{yu}U+B_{yu}$, where $A_{yu}=s_{y_\beta}/s_{u_\beta}$ and $B_{yu}=M_{y_\beta}-A_{yu}M_{u_\beta}$, then $Y=A_{yx}X+B_{yx}$, where $A_{yx}=A_{yu}/A_{xu}$, and $B_{yx}=B_{yu}-A_{yx}B_{xu}$. In order to insure that the conversion equation, $Y=A_{yx}X+B_{yx}$, has the appropriate generality, Form U must be a parallel form of X and Y if there is to be freedom in the choice of Groups α and β. If Form U is not parallel to X and Y, then Groups α and β must be drawn at random from the same population. Under conditions of random sampling, Lord (1950)

---

[19]A variant in the notation for the A and B values is introduced from this point on wherever necessary to avoid ambiguity. In general, A_{gh} and B_{gh} are the slope and intercept parameters, respectively, of the linear equation for converting scores from the scale of H to the scale of G, as follows: $G=A_{gh}H+B_{gh}$.

has shown that the variance error of equating by this method is given, approximately, by:

$$SE_{y^*}^2 = 4s_{y_\beta}^2(1 - r)\frac{z_x^2(1 + r) + 2}{N_t},$$ [41]

where it is assumed that $r = r_{xu_\alpha} = r_{yu_\beta}$. Comparison of equation 41 with equation 15 shows that this method of equating has four times the error variance of the counterbalanced method described as design II. Lord pointed out that half of this increase in error variance is attributable to the fact that in this method only half the examinees take each test, X or Y, whereas in design II all examinees take both tests. The other half of the increase in error variance arises from the fact that this method really involves two equatings instead of only one. Lord then pointed out that at the mean ($z_x = 0$) the error variance for this method is even larger than that for design I (administration of Forms X and Y to random halves of a total group; no additional equating test administered), unless r is at least .50. If r is zero, the error variance of this method is exactly twice that for design I. Even if r is somewhat greater than .50, the error variance in equation 41 will be larger than that in equation 10 if z_x is sufficiently large. This would indicate that if r is less than .50, it would be better to ignore all data relating to Form U and use the method of design I (assuming, of course, that Groups α and β are randomly chosen; this is essential) than to use the present method. Undoubtedly the added advantage of the data from Form U is more than offset by the fact that there are two equatings here instead of just one and therefore two sources of error.

2. Curvilinear analog

The curvilinear analog to the method described in the preceding section is clear. Forms X and U are equated by an equipercentile method, as are Forms Y and U. Then for each score on Form U the equivalent scores on X and Y are found, plotted, and smoothed to yield a conversion from X to Y.

B. Forms X and Y predicted by a common test

1. Linear procedure

If the same design of administration is carried out—Form X administered to Group α, Form Y administered to Group β, and Form U administered to both groups—it is possible to define as equivalent those scores on X and Y that are predicted by the same score on U. Thus if $\hat{X} = b_{xu}U + D_{xu}$, where $b_{xu} = r_{xu_\alpha}(s_{x_\alpha}/s_{u_\alpha})$ and $D_{xu} = M_{x_\alpha} - b_{xu}M_{u_\alpha}$, and if $\hat{Y} = b_{yu}U + D_{yu}$, where $b_{yu} = r_{yu_\beta}(s_{y_\beta}/s_{u_\beta})$ and $D_{yu} = M_{y_\beta} - b_{yu}M_{u_\beta}$, then $Y = AX + B$, where

$$A = b_{yu}/b_{xu} \qquad [42]$$

and

$$B = D_{yu} - AD_{xu}. \qquad [43]$$

The same considerations regarding the generality of results apply to this method as to the method just previously described. The administration of Form U must either precede the administration of both X and Y or it must follow them both. Form U must be parallel in function to X and Y if there is to be freedom in the choice of Groups α and β. However, if there is to be freedom in the choice of Form U, then Groups α and β must be randomly drawn from the same population.

   2. *Curvilinear analog*

   In the curvilinear adaptation, scatterplots of X on U and Y on U are drawn up. Means of the X arrays and means of the Y arrays are calculated for corresponding fixed values of U, plotted and smoothed. The resulting curve relating the points $M_{x.u}$ versus $M_{y.u}$ describes the relationship between Form X and Form Y.

   C. *Forms X and Y predicting a common test*

   1. *Linear procedure*

   Again using the same design of administration—Form X administered to Group α, Form Y administered to Group β, and Form U administered to both groups—scores on X and Y are defined as equivalent if they predict, instead of being predicted by (as in the preceding definition) the same score on U. Thus if $\hat{U} = b_{ux}X + D_{ux}$, where $b_{ux} = r_{ux_\alpha}(s_{u_\alpha}/s_{x_\alpha})$ and $D_{ux} = M_{u_\alpha} - b_{ux}M_{x_\alpha}$, and if $\hat{U} = b_{uy}Y + D_{uy}$, where $b_{uy} = r_{uy_\beta}(s_{u_\beta}/s_{y_\beta})$ and $D_{uy} = M_{u_\beta} - b_{uy}M_{y_\beta}$, then $Y = AX + B$, where

$$A = b_{ux}/b_{uy} \qquad [44]$$

and

$$B = (D_{ux} - D_{uy})/b_{uy}. \qquad [45]$$

The same considerations regarding the choice of tests and groups and the same considerations regarding administrative procedure apply here as in the method just described where scores on Forms X and Y are predicted by scores on U.

   2. *Curvilinear analog*

   Here, too, scatterplots are drawn up, but this time of U on X and U on Y. Means of the U arrays are calculated and plotted for fixed values of X and also for fixed values of Y, yielding two curves which are then smoothed. Finally, values of X and values of Y are read from their corresponding graphs for the same values of U, plotted against each other, and smoothed.

There are undoubtedly many other variations in ways of dealing with the basic set of data described here. It would be expected, of course, that the most reliable and most generally applicable results would be those obtained from the maximum use of the available data, collected under appropriate and rigorous conditions.

Design VI: Methods of score equating based on item data

A. *Thurstone's absolute scaling method (Thurstone, 1925; also Fan, 1957)*

The method described here applies to the following situation: Group α takes Form X and Group β takes Form Y. Forms X and Y have a set of items in common for which difficulty values, p, have been obtained and converted to their corresponding normal deviates, z', which, unlike the p values, are expressed on a linear scale. Like all methods of score equating, this method assumes that Forms X and Y are parallel forms and therefore can be converted to a unique common scale. It also assumes that the distributions for Groups α and β would both be normal on this scale. For the present purpose the common scale is taken to be the scale of Y.

The purpose of the method is to find relationships between the sets of item difficulties for the two groups that will lead to a conversion from raw scores on Form X to raw scores on Form Y, as in the equation, $Y = AX + B$, where $A = s_{y_\alpha}/s_{x_\alpha} (= s_{y_\beta}/s_{x_\beta})$ and $B = M_{y_\alpha} - AM_{x_\alpha}$ $(= M_{y_\beta} - AM_{x_\beta})$. If it is assumed that the distribution of ability scores is normal within the Groups α and β, then the following statements can be written describing the scale value, Y_i, of any item i, on the scale of the ability represented by Y, assuming perfect correlation between item and ability:

$$z_{i_\alpha} = \frac{Y_i - M_{y_\alpha}}{s_{y_\alpha}}, \qquad [46]$$

and

$$z_{i_\beta} = \frac{Y_i - M_{y_\beta}}{s_{y_\beta}}, \qquad [47]$$

where M_{y_α}, M_{y_β}, and s_{y_α}, and s_{y_β} are the ability score means and standard deviations for Groups α and β, and z_{i_α} and z_{i_β} are the

118

standard-score values of the scale position of item i for Groups α and β, respectively. Setting 46 and 47 equal,

$$z_{i_\beta} = (s_{y_\alpha}/s_{y_\beta})z_{i_\alpha} + \frac{M_{y_\alpha} - M_{y_\beta}}{s_{y_\beta}}. \qquad [48]$$

If, also, a bivariate plot of the normal deviates, z'_{i_β} versus z'_{i_α}, is constructed, the relationship between them can be expressed as:

$$z'_{i_\beta} = (s'_\beta/s'_\alpha)z'_{i_\alpha} + M'_\beta - (s'_\beta/s'_\alpha)M'_\alpha, \qquad [49]$$

where M'_α, M'_β, s'_α, and s'_β are the means and standard deviations of the normal deviates for the two groups.

Assuming that 48 and 49 are alternative expressions of the same relationship, it is concluded that the slopes are equal, i.e., that

$$s_{y_\alpha}/s_{y_\beta} = s'_\beta/s'_\alpha, \qquad [50]$$

and that the intercepts are equal, i.e., that

$$(M_{y_\alpha} - M_{y_\beta})/s_{y_\beta} = M'_\beta - (s'_\beta/s'_\alpha)M'_\alpha. \qquad [51]$$

From equations 50 and 51 the estimated values, $\hat{s}_{y_\alpha}$ and $\hat{M}_{y_\alpha}$, may be obtained for the calculation of the values of the slope, $A = \hat{s}_{y_\alpha}/s_{x_\alpha}$, and the intercept, $B = \hat{M}_{y_\alpha} - A M_{x_\alpha}$, of the conversion equation relating raw scores on Form X to raw scores on Form Y: $\hat{s}_{y_\alpha} = s_{y_\beta}(s'_\beta/s'_\alpha)$ and $\hat{M}_{y_\alpha} - s_{y_\beta}[M'_\beta - (s'_\beta/s'_\alpha)M'_\alpha] + M_{y_\beta}$.

Ordinarily, the plot of points for z'_{i_α} versus z'_{i_β} will form a narrow linear elliptical pattern, verifying (by the fact that it is linear) that the distributions of Groups α and β can be normalized on the same scale and indicating, by the high correlation represented by the tight swarm of points, that the items have the same "meaning" or represent the same "task" for the two groups of individuals. Indeed, the pattern of these points, represented analytically as the item-group interaction, will reveal the presence of items that may be "biased" toward one of the two groups. The technique of examining the bivariate plot of item difficulties, either graphically or analytically, has proved to be an extremely useful tool in the search for cultural bias in test items (Cleary & Hilton, 1966), in the investigation of curricular differences in achievement test items (Angoff, 1971), and in item calibration (Thurstone, 1947).

The principal test of the validity of the Thurstone method of absolute scaling is the extent to which equations 48 and 49 are indeed representations of the same line. With the use of actual data taken from the administration of a power test to widely different subgroups of examinees, and also with fictitious but perfectly consistent item and score data for groups of different ability, Fan (1957) compared the results that would be obtained from score data appropriate to equation 48 and from item data, based on the same examinees, appropriate to equation 49 and found that the results were indeed quite different. These differences, he pointed out, could not be attributed to sampling error in the data but necessarily resulted from the attempt to equate test forms that are administered to groups of different ability.

It is possible that the failure of the Thurstone method (of calibrating tests through item statistics) to deal adequately with groups that are substantially different is due to the obviously untenable assumption that the item-ability (or item-test) correlations are unity. On the other hand, Torgerson (1958, p. 395) points out that the requirement of perfectly discriminating items is unnecessarily restrictive. The model, he goes on to say, will fit the data, assuming only that the item characteristic curves are normal ogives and that the correlations of the items with the underlying ability are all equal. Clearly, this latter assumption especially, like the assumption of perfect item-test correlations, is also rarely, if ever, met in practice. As a result, the absolute scaling method as applied to item data, although important from a theoretical and historical point of view, is not useful in practice except when the distributions of the groups are very nearly alike, at least in the first two moments.

B. *Swineford-Fan method of equating*

Like the Thurstone method of absolute scaling (i.e., equating) the Swineford-Fan procedure (Swineford & Fan, 1957) is based on estimations made from a set of items common to two forms of the same test, Form X and Form Y, where Form X is administered to Group α and Form Y is administered to Group β. In order to calculate the slope, $A = s_{y_\alpha}/s_{x_\alpha}$, and intercept, $B = M_{y_\alpha} - AM_{x_\alpha}$, of the equation, $Y = AX + B$, relating Form X to Form Y, it is necessary first to estimate M_{y_α} and s_{y_α}.

The estimation process derives from the fact that for a test, W, of n items the raw (rights) score mean and standard deviation can be expressed in terms of item statistics as follows:

$$M_w = \sum_{i=1}^{n} p_i, \qquad [52]$$

and

$$s_w = \sum_{i=1}^{n} p_i d_i, \qquad [53]$$

where

p_i = proportion of correct responses for item i,

$d_i = (M_i - M_w)/s_w$, and

M_i = mean raw test score of those answering item i correctly.

Equation 53 comes from Gulliksen (1950, chap. 21) in which it is shown (eq. 20, p. 377) that $s_w = \Sigma_{i=1}^{n} r_{iw} \sqrt{p_i q_i}$, where r_{iw} is the point-biserial item-test correlation, and (eq. 32, p. 387) $r_{iw} \sqrt{p_i q_i} = p_i(M_i - M_w)/s_w$.

If, for the set of common items, a bivariate plot is made of the normal deviate values, z_i', corresponding to the values, p_i, as observed in the two groups, a line may be drawn relating the z' values for the two groups, as follows:

$$z_\alpha' = (s_\alpha'/s_\beta')z_\beta' + M_\alpha' - (s_\alpha'/s_\beta')M_\beta', \qquad [54]$$

where, as before, M' and s' are the mean and standard deviation, respectively, of the z' values. Using this line the z_α' values may be estimated from the z_β' values for the *noncommon* items in Form Y. Converting the values of z' to values of p for all the items in Form Y—those estimated for Group α as well as those observed—and summing for all items in Form Y, an estimated value of M_{y_α} may be generated, as shown in equation 52.

Making a similar plot of the values d_i for the set of common items, it is similarly possible to develop a line relating the d values (which, it is noted, are independent of the metrics of the tests) for the two groups, as follows:

$$d_\alpha = (s_\alpha''/s_\beta'')d_\beta + M_\alpha'' - (s_\alpha''/s_\beta'')M_\beta'', \qquad [55]$$

where M'' and s'' are the mean and standard deviation, respectively, of the d values. Corresponding to the procedure followed with equation 54, equation 55 can be used to estimate the d values for the noncommon items in Form Y for Group α. Multiplying the observed values of d_i and p_i for the common items and the estimated values of d_i and p_i for all noncommon items in Form Y, and summing the products, it is possible, as shown in equation 53, to generate an estimated value of s_{y_α}. With the estimated values, $\hat{M}_{y_\alpha}$ and $\hat{s}_{y_\alpha}$, and the corresponding observed values, M_{x_α} and s_{x_α}, the conversion parameters are calculated for the equation, $Y = AX + B$.

Equating and Calibration Systems

Ordinarily, the standard error of equating, as shown in equations 10, 15, 22, and 41, is quite small in comparison with the standard error of measurement. However, as has already been pointed out, the error of equating appears in the conversion equation itself, and so it is transmitted to every score to which the equation is applied and affects the summary statistics of all scores very much in the manner of a bias. In this respect it is like the error in a norms distribution but *unlike* other kinds of statistical error, as, for example, the error of measurement in a mean, which tends to vanish as the sample size is increased. Thus, while the error of equating is small in relation to the error of a single test score, it can loom quite large in relation to the error in a mean and can seriously affect comparisons of group performance. Moreover, in any large testing program where many forms of the same test are produced and equated, the error of equating can become quite considerable, if left unchecked. If, for example, successive forms were each equated to their immediate predecessors in chain fashion, then the variance of equated scores for the most recent form in relation to the original form would be $m\mathrm{SE}_{y*}^2$ (where SE_{y*}^2 is the average variance error of any one equating process and m is the number of equating links in the chain). That is to say, the variance error in the entire system would increase directly as a function of the number of links, or equatings involved, and could become competitive in size even with the variance error of measurement in a single score. On the other hand, if the equating system were allowed to develop, not as a simple chain but without any plan, then it is entirely possible that separate "strains" or "families" of scales could develop, with the very likely result that two forms, contiguous with respect to the order of their appearance, could be quite distantly related in terms of the number of equating links between them, and as a result of equating error alone, could yield two scaled scores for a given ability level that differed much more than they would have if the forms had been schematically closer together.

In order to reduce the form-to-form equating errors and to work toward the development of a cohesive and internally consistent system, it is advisable to equate each new form, not to one, but to *two* previous forms, and to average the results. Say that Y is an old form for which there already exists an equation, $C = A_{cy}Y + B_{cy}$, permitting the conversion of raw scores to the reporting scale. If scores on the new form (X) are equated to raw scores on Form Y, resulting in the equation $Y = A_{yx}X + B_{yx}$, it becomes possible to develop the conversion, $C = A'_{cx}X + B'_{cx}$, relating Form X raw scores to the scale, simply by substituting one equation into the other: $A'_{cx} = A_{cy}A_{yx}$ and $B'_{cx} = A_{cy}B_{yx} + B_{cy}$. If Form X also is equated to a second old form, Z (for which there already exists the equation, $C = A_{cz}Z + B_{cz}$), resulting in the equation, $Z = A_{zx}X + B_{zx}$, it becomes possible to develop a second conversion, $C = A''_{cx}X + B''_{cx}$, also by substituting one equation into the other: $A''_{cx} = A_{cz}A_{zx}$ and $B''_{cx} = A_{cz}B_{zx} + B_{cz}$. If it is assumed that the characteristics of Form X will dictate its conversion parameters (the slope and intercept of the equation converting raw scores to scaled scores), then it also may be hypothesized there will be a unique "true" line relating Form X to the scale. The two conversion lines, $C = A'_{cx}X + B'_{cx}$ and $C = A''_{cx}X + B''_{cx}$, may then be regarded as two estimates of the true line and averaged if it appears that the differences between them are only random. (An "average" line may be determined by bisecting the angle between the lines or by averaging the A values and averaging the B values.) In a large-scale testing program, like the College Board's Scholastic Aptitude Test (SAT) used for admissions, where new forms of a test are introduced at frequent intervals, it is possible to erect a systematic network of equating linkages among the test forms by specifying the ways in which the pair of old forms would be chosen for the equating of each of the new forms. Such a plan was indeed worked out for the College Board program (McGee, 1961), designed to organize the linkages among the test forms in a "braiding" fashion, by which it was hoped to shorten the "equating distance" between every form and every other form and to knit the system more tightly together. If properly executed, such a plan tends to enhance the reliability of the conversion for any new form, and, in consequence of this greater reliability, it tends to enhance the equivalence or calibration of scores among forms.

Calibration of Tests at Different Levels of Ability

Some systems of tests are designed to permit the measurement of a set of abilities over a wide range of talent, as would be found over a series of age levels—for example, from early childhood to adolescence—or over a series of grade levels—from the elementary grades to college level. There are a number of systems of tests of this type, both tests that yield an IQ or grade equivalent—for example the Stanford-Binet, the Kuhlmann-Anderson, the Lorge-Thorndike, and the Iowa Tests of Basic Skills—and tests that do not—for example the Cooperative School and College Ability Test and Sequential Tests of Educational Progress.

If there were one very long test, appropriately constructed for the entire expanse of talent, then each examinee in the standardization group would take the same long test, and raw scores on that test could be scaled in one of the ways described earlier in this chapter (see section on scaling). However, to give each examinee the same long test is clearly uneconomical; since there would be so many items that would be clearly too easy for him and (or) so many items that would be clearly too difficult for him, it would be a waste of his time and effort for him to take them all. In some tests, like the Stanford-Binet (Terman & Merrill,

1960), each examinee takes only those items that differentiate for him, plus enough additional easy and difficult items to verify that he has truly exhausted the band of item difficulty that would provide adequate measurement of his ability. Once the "basal" and "empty" years have been established, it is assumed that the examinee would have passed all items below the basal year and would have failed all the items above the empty year, had he taken them. In other tests, like the Lorge-Thorndike Multi-Level Edition (Lorge et al., 1966), there is a series of eight tests, one test for each of eight levels. Each test consists of a group of modular units, or subtests, also graded in difficulty but more finely. As one proceeds from one test level to the next higher level, the easiest modular unit is dropped from the beginning of the test and a more difficult modular unit is added at the upper end. Thus, every one of the eight available test levels has a considerable proportion (80 percent) of items in common with the test level just below it and also with the test level just above it. (The exceptions to this, of course, are the lowest test level, which has items in common only with the levels above it, and the highest test level, which has items in common only with the levels below it.) In still other tests, like the Cooperative School and College Ability Test (SCAT) (1956), five mutually exclusive tests are available pitched at five spans of grade level.

Particularly in the case of tests like the Lorge-Thorndike and the SCAT, procedures have been developed for calibrating each test level with the other tests in the series in order to yield scores on one underlying scale. The different procedures have much in common, but there are many variations in approach. One such approach may be described as:

1. One test in the center of the series (say, V, W, X, Y, and Z) is chosen as the anchor, and the tests just above and just below it are calibrated to it. Scores on this test (Level X) are put on an arbitrary *interim scale* for the purposes of the calibration operations, simply by defining one score (say, 450) to correspond to the minimum raw score on the anchor form and another score (say, 550) to correspond to the maximum raw score on the anchor form, taking care to provide no less than one scaled score unit for each raw score unit on the anchor form. This operation yields the equation, $C = A_{cx}X + B_{cx}$, using the notation adopted earlier, where A_{cx} and B_{cx} are the slope and intercept, respectively, of the linear equation relating scores on Level X to the interim scale.

2. A set of common test material is constructed for purposes of the calibration. In the case of the Lorge-Thorndike Multi-Level Edition the common material appears as an integral part of the tests; in the case of other tests, like SCAT, common test material was prepared explicitly for

the calibration and administered along with the operational forms of SCAT, but not as an integral part of those forms. Preferably, the common material should contain items that will be sufficiently discriminating for the two groups for which the two adjacent test levels are appropriate.

3. A sample of students is chosen representing the group for whom the anchor test (Level X) is appropriate, and another sample is chosen representing the group for which the next level of test (say, Level Y, the level below it) is appropriate. The Level X test and the Level Y test are administered to random halves of both groups. (This is most easily accomplished by packaging the Level X test and the Level Y test in alternating order and distributing them to both groups.) If the common test material is separate, then it should be administered as an integral test to everyone in both groups and, of course, in the same order (preceding *or* following the operational test, X or Y).

4. Using equations 30 to 33, estimates of mean and variance are made for both levels for the combined group taking both levels. These estimates are then applied to equation 7, resulting in the equation, $X = A_{xy} Y + B_{xy}$. Substituting into the equation for converting raw scores on Level X to the interim scale results in the equation, $C = A_{cy} Y + B_{cy}$.

5. The process in steps 2 to 4 is repeated in order to calibrate Level Z to Level Y and, through Level Y, to the interim scale. In the same way, Level W is calibrated to Level X and, through it, to the scale; and Level V is calibrated to Level W and, through it, to the scale. The result of this process is a series of conversions to the interim scale, one conversion for each test level. If, for example, each of the series of five tests described here were to occupy 100 scaled score points on the interim scale and had 50 percent overlap with its neighbor, then the entire length of the interim scale could extend from 350 to 650—with Level Z extending from 350 to 450, Level Y from 400 to 500, Level X from 450 to 550, Level W from 500 to 600, and, finally, Level V from 550 to 650.

Once the articulation of these tests is accomplished, the attention of the test constructor can be turned to the questions of defining the final scale and providing norms. It is entirely possible that the scale adopted here for interim purposes would be satisfactory for permanent use. The advantages characteristic of such a scale already have been discussed in the section on scaling—especially that a scale defined nonnormatively gives maximum flexibility for providing a variety of normative data and for updating the norms at regular intervals. However, the same advantages, and more, would be characteristic of the scales developed by Lazarsfeld, Lord, Tucker, Birnbaum, and Rasch (also discussed in the section on scaling), which are highly superior to the interim scale discussed here, since they are based on the inherent psychometric properties of the tests themselves.

If an IQ scale is to be developed, then distributions of the interim scaled scores are prepared for a random sample of individuals at each age level. Normal deviates corresponding to the mid-percentile ranks are determined, multiplied by 16 (to give an IQ scale with a standard deviation of 16 at each age; they would be multiplied by 15 to give the scale a standard deviation of 15 at each age) and 100 is added to result in a scale with a mean of 100. This process provides a conversion from the interim scale to a normalized deviation IQ at each age level. Since the conversion from raw scores to the interim scale is already established for each level, it is possible to express the relationship between raw scores and deviation IQs directly, bypassing the interim scale.

Procedures similar to these can be applied to the computation of grade equivalents. The conversion to the interim scale is precisely the same as described, but the computation beyond that point is different. After the norms are collected separately by grade, the mean or median interim scaled score is computed at each grade level, and a smooth curve is drawn relating grade and score, and scores are recorded to tenths of a grade. Here too, since the conversion from raw scores to the interim scale is already established for each test level, it is possible to express the relationship between raw scores and grade equivalents directly, bypassing the interim scale.

There are numerous detailed variations possible in this calibration. Linear equations other than those following the Tucker derivation are possible. Also, the various test levels can be equated by one of the equipercentile methods. Or, raw scores on the adjacent test levels can be normalized, and the normalized scores equated by any one of the appropriate linear procedures described in this section. As a result of either of these two latter classes of methods there will be a curvilinear transformation from raw to interim scores. As is often true with procedures that depend on locally determined statistics (e.g., percentiles), extrapolation may be necessary at the extremes of each of the raw score scales where there are insufficient data to define the transformation in detail.

A principal concern in this calibration across tests of different levels is that the psychological function measured may change from level to level, in which case the notion of a single reference scale, equally appropriate throughout the series of levels, tends to lose its meaning. Generally speaking, this problem is more serious for tests which are highly dependent on the curriculum and on school subjects that may be introduced at different points in time as a function of local custom and decisions and developed through the grades at different rates and sequences. It is probably not as serious for tests of general intellectual abilities that are acquired and developed outside the classroom.

4. Comparable Scores

Unlike the problem of *equivalent* scores, which is restricted to the case of parallel forms of a test, that is, to tests of the same psychological function, the problem of *comparable* scores may be thought of quite simply as the problem of "equating" tests of *different* psychological function. Ordinarily, two tests are considered to have been made comparable *with respect to a particular group of examinees* if their distributions of scores are identical (Frequently, comparable scores are defined, not in terms of the shapes of the distributions—i.e., all standardized moments—but in terms of the mean and standard deviation alone.) As the definition indicates, score scales are comparable only with respect to a specific group tested under specific conditions. Comparability will also hold reasonably well with respect to other groups, but only if those other groups are drawn from the same population as the group on which comparability was originally established. Thus, comparable scores for two tests will differ, depending on at least three considerations:

1. *The nature of the group.* Different reference groups will yield different relationships between the two tests. This consideration is basic and will be discussed in more detail.

2. *The definition of comparability.* Different definitions of comparability will yield different relationships. For example, it was just mentioned above that two tests could be considered comparable if their distributions of scores are identical. This is one definition. Another definition is that two tests are considered comparable if the distributions of their *true scores* are identical. If the two tests are unequally reliable, then these two definitions will yield different types of comparability.

3. *The method of deriving the comparability.* Different methods of deriving comparable scores may yield quite different results.

Sometimes the distinction between *definition* of comparability and *method* of deriving comparable scores is unclear, and the two may be considered as essentially equivalent. Whatever the definition or method of comparability, the relationship is meaningful *only* with respect to a *single* particular group or population of individuals or to random samples drawn from a single population.

The methods of establishing tables of comparable scores between tests are almost as numerous as the methods of equating scores and include both linear and curvilinear procedures. Although the methods discussed here are principally the linear methods, it should be understood that whenever a linear method is appropriate, the curvilinear analog, if there is one, is similarly appropriate. In fact, in some instances, when the shapes of the raw score distributions differ substantially, the curvilinear approach may be preferable.

Probably the most common procedure of defining comparability is simply to administer the two or more tests (frequently a battery of tests) to a common basic reference group and to scale the tests in such a way that the mean and standard deviation have the same numerical values, respectively, on each of the various tests. Sometimes, in addition, the distributions are normalized. Scores on the various tests of the battery then are used to plot profiles for purposes of differential diagnosis, remediation, and placement.

Some of the methods of equating (equivalent scores) are not appropriate for defining comparability because they call for some basic assumptions that are necessarily excluded in the problem of comparable scores. These include the methods of calibration attributable to Levine (1955), since they all assume not only that Forms X and Y are parallel (as do all methods of equating) but also that the equating test, Form U, is parallel in function to both X and Y. Clearly, if X and Y are not parallel, U cannot be parallel to both of them.

In general, the methods that make use of an equating test, or those that make use of a set of common items that are interspersed throughout the tests, have their limitations for deriving systems of comparable scores for the very reason that X and Y are tests of different function. For example, the method of absolute scaling (Thurstone, 1925) assumes that the correlations between the common items and the total test are perfect. Even if this assumption could be defended for Tests X and Y that are parallel, it could not be defended for tests of different function. Items that correlate perfectly with X cannot correlate perfectly with Y if X and Y themselves do not correlate perfectly.

Very likely the most defensible procedure for deriving comparable scores is that described under design I, in which Tests (note: *here* they are *not* test forms) X and Y are administered to random halves of a group that is drawn, also at random, from a defined population. The methods of design III (Lord, 1955a) and design IV derived by Tucker (Gulliksen, 1950; Angoff, 1961a), and probably the methods described under design V (other methods involving score data) are also appropriate, but with some reservations that may be regarded as further restrictions on the generality with which a table of comparable scores may be applied and used. Specifically, if Tests X and Y are tests that measure distinctly different characteristics, then in all likelihood Test U, the anchor or equating test, will not correlate equally with them.

Consequently, the second terms in equations 18 to 21, and also in equations 30 to 33 will be unequally regressed. This will not ordinarily pose a problem except for the fact that the estimations of mean and variance for the test with the lower correlation with Test U will be relatively unreliable and biased with respect to the estimations for the other test. In the equating model, on the other hand, where $r_{xu} = r_{yu}$, the estimations for both tests are equally regressed.

Some of the variations of the procedure involving the use of common tests may be appropriate here too: for example, establishing the comparability of three or more tests simultaneously, using multiple predictors, and using a *quasi-common* equating test (see pp. 104–109; also p. 112).

By way of illustration, it may be useful to describe the method of equating that makes use of all three of the foregoing variations but as applied to the problem of comparable scores. Consider a testing battery, like the one used in the College Board Admissions Testing Program (also the Graduate Record Examinations Program), in which all examinees take a common core of tests, say both the Verbal and the Mathematical sections of the SAT, and in addition, one or more of the various Achievement Tests of their own choosing in specific subject-matter areas. One procedure that is sometimes thought appropriate for making the scales on the various tests comparable is to define all the means and standard deviations at some convenient pair of numbers (in the case of the College Board program, at 500 and 100, respectively) for the particular group of people taking each test. (Other types of comparability involve the definition of *all* the moments of the distribution, not only the first two.) However, assuming—as is often the case—that the groups of people taking the various tests are drawn from different populations, such a procedure would fail to satisfy the fundamental definition of comparability, which is that certain agreed-upon moments of the distributions of scores on the two tests be identical *with respect to a particular (single) group of examinees*. The choice of the same system of numbers for all the tests would only ensure that the scales *appear* to be comparable. But since they would not be comparable in the accepted sense, their apparent comparability would necessarily be false and misleading.

The example of the College Board Admissions Testing Program is helpful in this context because it possesses the characteristics that make for a relatively complex system of comparable scores. The procedure that has been followed there has two basic omponents, the comparability of the two sections of the SAT and the comparability of the various Achievement Tests with one another and with the SAT. In the case of the SAT all candidates, or virtually all candidates, take both the Verbal and the Mathematical sections. The exceptions are extremely rare and can easily be identified and removed from the standardization group. Thus it was a reasonable thing to define the mean and standard deviation for both the Verbal and Mathematical sections as 500 and 100 respectively for a particular standardization group. The group taken for this purpose consisted of those tested at the April 1941 administration of the SAT. As a result of this procedure comparability is established between Verbal and Mathematical in the linear sense (since only the first two moments are so defined) and without approximation, since both tests are taken by the same group of examinees.[20]

The problem of the Achievement Tests is another matter, however. Here, the choice of test is left to the examinee and to the college of application, which, of course, also represents a matter of choice for the examinee. Since the tests chosen by the examinees are those on which they feel they are most likely to do well, it is expected that, because of this self-selection, there would be differences in the abilities of the groups that elect to take the various tests, differences that are likely to be evident in the scores on the SAT. Since, also, the scores that are reported on the various tests of the Achievement Test battery are used more or less interchangeably by many of the colleges in evaluating the abilities of their applicants, it becomes necessary to introduce as precise a comparability among the test scales as possible, that is to say, to adjust the scales for the various tests in order to reflect the levels and dispersions of the groups of candidates who choose to take them. In another, but closely related, sense, it is important to insure that the principal requirement of the definition of comparability be satisfied, that the moments of the distributions of scores be defined in terms of the *same reference group*. Since, in this situation, the tests are not all taken by all the members of the reference group, it becomes necessary to make estimations. The appropriate equations for these estimations are similar to those described briefly above for the situation where more than two forms (say X, Y, and Z) of a test are being equated and where estimates of raw score mean and variance are made for the combined group, all of whom take the equating test (see pp. 107–108 and 112). Additional variations are: (*a*) that not one equating test, but two, are used in multiple combination; and (*b*) that the students do not necessarily all take precisely the same form of SAT-Verbal or the same form of SAT-Mathematical. Thus, the SAT is used in the sense of a *quasi-*

[20]Actually there is a degree of approximation here. The SAT-Verbal was defined as described above, in April 1941; the SAT-Mathematical was not defined until April 1942, and this was done by assigning it the same mean and standard deviation as were found on the SAT-Verbal at that April 1942 administration.

common test. Following the form given in equations 23 to 26, which may be extended to as many tests and corresponding test groups as necessary, estimates are made of the raw score mean and variance on each of the Achievement Tests for the same standard reference group. This group is defined as one having a mean of 500 and standard deviation of 100 on both SAT-Verbal and SAT-Mathematical, and a Verbal-Mathematical covariance of 4,000. After these estimates are made, each pair of estimates (mean and variance) is defined as 500 and 10,000 (that is, 100 for the standard deviation) in accordance with equation 7 (Schultz & Angoff, 1956; also Angoff, 1961a).

It should be noted that from the point of view of their derivation, equations 23 to 26 are extensions of equations 18 to 21, which depend on the assumption that the subgroups taking the different forms are only randomly different. The comparable scores problem that is being considered here necessarily fails to satisfy that assumption, and, therefore, the estimates required for it must be derived from other assumptions, such as those basic to equations 30 to 33. However, in spite of these differences in assumptions, equations 23 to 26 are computationally precisely equivalent to the formulas needed for the comparable scores problem and may be considered appropriate for that use.

The scaling of the four original language Achievement Tests of the College Board (French, German, Latin, and Spanish) will illustrate the way in which the use of two anchor test variables may be extended to three. In a study conducted by L. R Tucker (Angoff, 1961b) data were collected that made it clear that the various foreign languages were studied for characteristically different amounts of time in secondary school. In order to reflect its role in the comparability among the language Achievement Tests, the number of years of language study was therefore added to SAT-Verbal and SAT-Mathematical as a third "anchor test" and used in equations involving three predictors, as shown in equations 56 and 57. These equations, providing estimates of mean and variance for the standard reference group on language test X, for example, are computationally parallel to equations 23 and 25, respectively, but extended to three variables.

$$
\begin{aligned}
\hat{\mu}_x = M_{x_\alpha} &+ b_{xv \cdot mn_\alpha}(\mu_v - M_{v_\alpha}) \\
&+ b_{xm \cdot vn_\alpha}(\mu_m - M_{m_\alpha}) \\
&+ b_{xn \cdot vm_\alpha}(\mu_n - M_{n_\alpha}),
\end{aligned}
\tag{56}
$$

and

$$\hat{\sigma}_x^2 = s_{x_\alpha}^2 + b_{xv \cdot mn_\alpha}^2 (\sigma_v^2 - s_{v_\alpha}^2)$$
$$+ b_{xm \cdot vn_\alpha}^2 (\sigma_m^2 - s_{m_\alpha}^2)$$
$$+ b_{xn \cdot vm_\alpha}^2 (\sigma_n^2 - s_{n_\alpha}^2)$$
$$+ 2b_{xv \cdot mn_\alpha} b_{xm \cdot vn_\alpha} (\sigma_{vm} - s_{vm_a})$$
$$+ 2b_{xv \cdot mn_\alpha} b_{xn \cdot vm_\alpha} (\sigma_{vn} - s_{vn_\alpha})$$
$$+ 2b_{xm \cdot vn_\alpha} b_{xn \cdot vm_\alpha} (\sigma_{mn} - s_{mn_\alpha}), \tag{57}$$

where n, the only new symbol used here, refers to the number of years of language training. Clearly, not all the members of the standard reference group had chosen to take a foreign language test, and population values involving years of language training were not available for them. However, since the matrix of the means, the variances, and the covariance for SAT-Verbal and SAT-Mathematical for the total *observed* group taking one or more languages was found to be very close to the population values (500, 10,000, and 4,000, respectively), the statistics involving years of language training (n) observed for the total group studying any one (or more than one) language were taken as population values for the purposes of equations 56 and 57.

If the desired definition of comparability involves all moments, not only the first two, analogous curvilinear methods that are applicable to the problem of optional tests and make use of the relationship with an anchor test can be worked out, corresponding to the curvilinear method of equating outlined in design IV about (p. 113). It also should be observed here that another procedure similar in intent to the procedure just described is Flanagan's scaled score system for the Cooperative Tests (Flanagan, 1939), which made use of the Stanford Achievement Test and the Otis Self-Administering Test of Mental Ability as "anchor" tests for the "50-point" for each of the Cooperative Achievement Tests. (See the section on scaling.)

One of the characteristics of the College Board method stems from the fact that correlations between the Achievement Tests and the SAT vary from test to test, with the result that the estimates of mean and variance given in equations 23 to 26 are affected by the *different amounts of regression* of the parenthetical terms as well as by the values of the parenthetical terms themselves. This differential regression in turn affects the placement of the scale for each test on the underlying scale structure for the entire battery. On the other hand, such a result is precisely what should occur, since information on the anchor test (the SAT) should be used only to the extent that it is relevant to performance on the subject-matter test.

133

There is one type of comparability that is particularly applicable to selection situations in which scores on different tests are available for different subgroups of the applicant body. In some such situations the applicants may have the choice of taking one or another of the selection tests. In other situations, as in bilingual cultures, where the tests are not equally appropriate for all applicants, there is in effect no choice possible for many applicants; the situation essentially determines the choice of test for them. Nevertheless, once accepted, the students are called upon to engage in a mixed competition in which there is an attempt made to disregard linguistic and cultural differences among students and to evaluate their performances in terms of what purports, at least, to be a common scale. In such situations, scores on the two (or more) tests may be made comparable by defining as "equivalent" those scores on the two (or more) tests that predict the same score on the criterion measure. The relationship used for this comparability is one of those given earlier in the section on equating and calibration for the same situation but involving parallel forms: $Y = AX + B$, where $A = b_{ux}/b_{uy}$ and

$$B = \frac{1}{b_{uy}} (D_{ux} - D_{uy}),$$

where $D_{ux} = M_{u_\alpha} - b_{ux} M_{x_\alpha}$ and $D_{uy} = M_{u_\beta} - b_{uy} M_{y_\beta}$ (equations 44 and 45).

Ideally, the two tests should correlate equally with the criterion. If they correlate unequally with the criterion then those applicants who offer as part of their credentials the test with the higher correlation and who score low on their test will be disadvantaged relative to the applicants who are at the same rank position but who offer the other test for admission. On the other hand, if they score high on their test they will be at an advantage relative to the applicants at the same rank position who offer the other test.

Scores on two tests may also be defined as comparable if they are *predicted* by the same score on a third variable. This procedure would be appropriate if one attempted, for example, to establish comparability among the grading systems employed in the various departments of a university and/or in various universities. In this situation, the test that had been administered for selection or just after matriculation at the university (or universities) might be used as the anchor test. The relationship for this comparability was also given in the section on equating and calibration, involving parallel forms (equations 42 and 43): $Y = AX + B$, where $A = b_{yu}/b_{xu}$ and $B = D_{yu} - AD_{xu}$, and where $D_{xu} = M_{x_\alpha} - b_{xu} M_{u_\alpha}$ with $D_{yu} = M_{y_\beta} - b_{yu} M_{u_\beta}$. Here, too, the comparability is affected by the difference in the correlations, r_{xu} and r_{yu}, but the advantages and disadvantages to the applicant go in the opposite direction. A student who takes the test with the *higher* correlation with the third variable and scores low on his test will have an advantage over those who are at the same rank position but who offer the other test. On the other hand, if that student scores high on his test he will be disadvantaged relative to the students at the same rank position who take the other test.

There is another method of defining comparability which appears to be direct and easy to apply and comprehend but which has grave limitations. This is the method that defines as the comparable Y score for each value of X the score on variable Y that would be predicted for that X score in the usual regression sense, that is by the equation, $Y = AX + B$, where $A = b_{yx}$ and $B = M_y - b_{yx}M_x$. The difficulty with this procedure is that scores on Test Y will therefore be regressed relative to the original distribution of Y scores; that is, they will have a reduced standard deviation, not equal to s_y, but equal to $r_{xy}s_y$ instead. The lower the correlation between Tests X and Y, the narrower will be the distribution of predicted Y scores. If the purpose of deriving comparable scores, as would probably be the case with this method, is to merge and compare scores earned on Test Y by some individuals with Y scores converted from Test X, taken by other individuals, then clearly this method is inappropriate. Moreover, it necessarily introduces bias, since, as a result of the regression method, individuals scoring below the mean on Test X would be given higher scores on Test Y, closer to the mean; and individuals scoring above the mean on Test X would be given lower scores on Test Y, also closer to the mean. Thus, if applicants were given the option, say in a selection competition, of taking Test X or Test Y, it would be to an applicant's best—and unfair—advantage to take Test X if he were a low-ability student and to take Test Y if he were a high-ability student. For obvious reasons, any procedure that is susceptible to strategic manipulations unrelated to the applicant's ability should be avoided. Finally, it should be pointed out that this regression method as a method of comparability suffers from the fact that its solution is not uniquely given. Rather than one, there are two lines possible, each unidirectional, one for predicting Y from X and the other for predicting X from Y. These lines are often equally defensible and appropriate, and for that reason they do not permit a clear choice. Yet they serve separate purposes and they yield different results. For example, the best estimate, by this procedure, of a person's score on Test Y, given his score of 74 on Test X, may be 68, but unless the correlation between Tests X and Y is perfect, the best estimate of his score on Test X, given that his score on

Test Y is 68, is *not* 74. Because of the lack of symmetry in this method (i.e., two separate unidirectional lines) and because of the regression effect, which does not permit the merging of obtained and converted scores, it would probably be advisable to avoid using this method of deriving comparable scores.

There appear to be two principal purposes for which comparable scores are derived. One is to merge and compare, and otherwise treat as interchangeable, scores on different tests for different examinees. Typical examples of comparability that serve this purpose are those derived for the different Advanced Tests of the Graduate Record Examinations, the different Achievement Tests of the College Board, and aptitude and achievement tests that are couched in different languages for students of different language background. The other purpose is to develop profiles across a battery of tests of different function. These profiles are used to study the patterns of performance for individuals and to identify relative strengths and weaknesses in different areas, presumably for differential diagnosis, guidance, and placement.

Whatever the purpose of the comparable scores, normative or ipsative, it is crucial to keep in mind the characteristics of the group on which the comparability is established and to interpret the results for individuals in terms of that group. It is meaningless to ask in the abstract whether a person is a better athlete than a student, whether he is more handsome than intelligent, more heavy than tall, or indeed, better in verbal than in mathematical tasks. It is quite meaningful, however, to ask these questions about his characteristics *in relation to a particular reference group*. But it must be kept in mind that, depending on the reference group that is chosen, the conclusions drawn from the comparison could be quite different. Thus an individual could be "better in verbal than in mathematical" if he is being compared with a male reference group but "better in mathematical than verbal" if he is being compared with a female reference group. This nonuniqueness of comparable scores derives from the fact that the measures in question are measures of different functions; there is no unique single conversion table that can be derived for tests of different functions, and there is no single conversion table that is applicable to all types of groups. This is so for the reason that different types of groups necessarily show different types of profiles, i.e., patterns of means, on tests of different functions. Indeed, because they reveal group characteristics and are closely dependent on the groups on which they are based, conversions across tests of different functions are themselves another way of expressing group profiles.

The matter of "equating" nonparallel tests has been reviewed in some detail by Angoff (1966). As was pointed out, here too, the problem of conversion from one form to a parallel[21] form of a test may be thought of simply as a problem of transforming systems of units, directly analogous to the conversion of Celsius to Fahrenheit, centimeters to inches, and so on. This kind of conversion, across systems of units for two instruments that measure precisely the same function, is unique. There is only one conversion, except for random error, however it is derived and however it is applied. But in the case of comparable scores for tests of different function, there would be as many conversions as there are groups for whom the tests are appropriate and as many conversions as there are situations for which the tests are appropriate. As Flanagan (1951) has pointed out, even two tests that purported to measure competence in the same subject (say, biology) but differed in emphasis, might show a pattern of performance for students in New York that was quite different from the pattern they exhibited for students in Los Angeles, and this pattern might well be a reflection of the patterns of curricular emphasis in the two cities.

The failure of nonparallel tests to yield a single set of comparable scores is apparent too when one considers a number of tests, each designed to measure competence in a different subject-matter area (e.g., spelling, arithmetic, reading, social studies) but over a range of grade levels. If one were to establish a system of comparable scores for these tests based on a group of students at grade 3, one would almost necessarily find that the scores were no longer comparable at grades 4 and 5 and still further in disagreement at grades 6, 7, and 8. The failure of the system to retain its comparability throughout the grades is the inevitable result of different growth rates, however the comparability is defined, and the differential growth rates are themselves, as Lindquist (1953) has pointed out, necessarily the result of arbitrary decisions to introduce the subject-matter concepts in the grades at certain fixed points in time and to progress in the subjects in a particular sequence at a particular rate. Any change in the pedagogic pattern, also arbitrary, would render entirely inapplicable whatever system of comparability had been established and would call for a totally new derivation in terms of the new pedagogic pattern.

Although tables of comparable scores bring with them problems that exist over and beyond the problems of equated scores for tests of similar

[21]As mentioned earlier in the section on equating and calibration, the operational definition of parallelism here is essentially the one developed by Wilks (1946) and extended by Votaw (1948): two tests may be considered parallel if, after conversion to the same scale, their means, standard deviations, and correlations with any and all outside criteria are equal (Gulliksen, 1950).

function, they are nevertheless extremely useful, indeed indispensable in many situations. Nevertheless, it is easy to overlook their sources of error. Some of these errors are random and are associated with any equating enterprise; others are associated with the fact that they deal with tests of different function and, because they are systematic and predictable, can only be taken as errors of bias.

Frequently the situation is one in which the tests and the use for which the table of comparable scores is required cannot be questioned or altered but must be dealt with directly. In such instances it may be possible at least to choose the kind of group to use in forming a conversion table. Three such groups are: (a) the national norms group; (b) a set of differentiated norms groups; and (c) the local norms group. Comparable scores based on a "sample of convenience," one for which data just happen to be available, are of little, if any, value.

Of the various kinds of comparable scores, the one based on differentiated norms is probably the most defensible. This procedure will yield a number of conversion tables, each based on, and appropriate for, a different norms group. Each conversion, like a profile, will be descriptive of the group on which it is based and applicable only to that group. The user will be forced to choose the appropriate table with care, keeping in mind the group for which he intends to use it and the purpose for which it is to be applied.

The local norms approach to comparable scores is similar to the one involving differentiated norms and is in general as highly recommended for the purpose of comparable scores as are local norms distributions themselves for the purpose of evaluating relative status. Here the cautions that need to be exercised are: (a) that the group has not been directly selected on either of the scores involved in the conversion; (b) that there are sufficient cases to yield reliable conversions; and (c) that the conversions be applied only in the institution (school or college) where they were developed or in institutions known to be similar to it.

The national norms approach is probably the least satisfactory of all, except when the tests in question are closely similar in function. Its principal advantage, however, is that it is the most readily applied method of obtaining rough conversion tables, if for no other reason than the fact that national norms for tests are generally readily available. The significant concern here is that the norms groups for the various tests may not have been selected in the same fashion in order to satisfy, even approximately, the requirement that the reference group for all tests be the same, or at least, randomly equivalent. The sources of unreliability in norms samples are numerous enough and large enough to introduce serious errors in tables of comparable scores.

If the methods of equating parallel forms are adapted to the problem of comparable scores for nonparallel tests, then it is pertinent to ask: (*a*) How similar are the tests for which comparable scores are to be developed? (*b*) How appropriate is the group on which the table of comparable scores is based when one considers the person or the group for whom the table is to be used? Once these questions are answered it would then be necessary to consider the purpose for which the table is to be used and the nature of the decisions that would be based on it in order to evaluate the degree of error that could be tolerated. Clearly, for some decisions, those that are not crucial and those that can be corrected if later found to be incorrect, the demand for precision is not great, while for other decisions and uses, those in which the careers of individuals are at stake, only the highest degree of precision is permitted. Each situation must be evaluated on its own merit, with full awareness that statistical solutions are fundamentally no more precise than the data they are based on and no more defensible than the methods used to derive them and the assumptions on which they are based.

REFERENCES

Angoff, W. H. Test reliability and effective test length. *Psychometrika,* 1953, **18**, 1–14.

Angoff, W. H. Measurement and scaling. In C. W. Harris (Ed.), *Encyclopedia of educational research.* (3rd ed.) New York: Macmillan, 1960. Pp. 807–817.

Angoff, W. H. Basic equations in scaling and equating. In S. S. Wilks (Ed.), *Scaling and equating College Board tests.* Princeton, N.J.: Educational Testing Service, 1961. Pp. 120–129.(a)

Angoff, W. H. Language training study: 1947. In S. S. Wilks (Ed.), *Scaling and equating College Board tests.* Princeton, N.J.: Educational Testing Service, 1961. Pp. 130–143.(b)

Angoff, W. H. Scales with nonmeaningful origins and units of measurement. Symposium: Standard scores for aptitude and achievement tests. *Educational and Psychological Measurement,* 1962, **22**, 27–34.

Angoff, W. H. Can useful general-purpose equivalency tables be prepared for different college admissions tests? In A. Anastasi (Ed.), *Testing problems in perspective.* Washington: American Council on Education, 1966. Pp. 251–264.

Angoff, W. H. How we calibrate College Board scores. *College Board Review,* 1968, No. 68, 11–14.

Angoff, W. H. (Ed.) *The College Board technical manual: A description of research and development for the College Board Scholastic Aptitude Test and Achievement Tests.* Princeton, N.J.: Educational Testing Service, 1971.

Angoff, W. H. Test scores and norms. In L. C. Deighton (Ed.), *Encyclopedia of Education.* New York: Macmillan, 1971. Pp. 153–165.

Angoff, W. H., & Waite, A. Study of double part-score equating for the Scholastic Aptitude Test. In S. S. Wilks (Ed.), *Scaling and Equating College Board Tests.* Princeton, N.J.: Educational Testing Service, 1961. Pp. 73–85.

Beggs, D. L., & Hieronymus, A. N. Uniformity of growth in the basic skills throughout the school year and during the summer. *Journal of Educational Measurement,* 1968, **5,** 91–97.

Birnbaum, A. Chaps. 17–20. In Lord, F. M., & Novick, M. R. *Statistical theories of mental test scores.* Reading, Mass.: Addison-Wesley Publishing Co., 1968.

Cattell, R. B. Psychological measurement: Normative, ipsative, interactive. *Psychological Review,* 1944, **51,** 292–303.

Cleary, T. A., & Hilton, T. L. An investigation of item bias. *Educational and Psychological Measurement,* 1968, **28,** 61–75.

Conrad, H. S. Norms. In W. S. Monroe (Ed.), *Encyclopedia of educational research.* (Rev. ed.) New York: Macmillan, 1950. Pp. 795–802.

Cooperative School and College Ability Tests: Manual for interpreting scores. Princeton, N.J.: Educational Testing Service, 1956.

Cooperative School and College Ability Tests: Handbook for SCAT series II. Princeton, N.J.: Educational Testing Service, 1967. 54 pp.

Cornell, F. G. Sampling methods. In C. W. Harris (Ed.), *Encyclopedia of educational research.* (3rd ed.) New York: Macmillan, 1960. Pp. 1181–1183.

Cureton, E. E. The accomplishment quotient technic. *Journal of Experimental Education,* 1937, **5,** 315–326.

Cureton, E. E. Minimum requirements in establishing and reporting norms on educational tests. *Harvard Educational Review,* 1941, **11,** 287–300.

Cureton, E. E., & Tukey, J. W. Smoothing frequency distributions, equating tests, and preparing norms. *American Psychologist,* 1951, **6,** 404. (Abstract)

Davenport, K. S., & Remmers, H. H. Factors in state characteristics related to average A-12 V-12 test scores. *Journal of Educational Psychology,* 1950, **41,** 110–115.

Ebel, R. L. Content standard test scores. Symposium: Standard scores for aptitude and achievement tests. *Educational and Psychological Measurement,* 1962, **22,** 15–25.

Fan, C.-t. On the applications of the method of absolute scaling. *Psychometrika,* 1957, **22,** 175–183.

Flanagan, J. C. *The Cooperative Achievement Tests: A bulletin reporting the basic principles and procedures used in the development of their system of scaled scores.* New York: American Council on Education, Cooperative Test Service, 1939.

Flanagan, J. C. (Ed.) *The aviation psychology program in the Army Air Forces.* (Report No. 1) Washington: Government Printing Office, 1948.

Flanagan, J. C. Units, scores, and norms. In E. F. Lindquist (Ed.), *Educational measurement.* Washington: American Council on Education, 1951. Pp. 695–763,

Flanagan, J. C. Selecting appropriate score scales for tests. (Discussion) In *Proceedings of the 1952 Invitational Conference on Testing Problems.* Princeton, N.J.: Educational Testing Service, 1953. Pp. 29–33.

Flanagan, J. C. Symposium: Standard scores for achievement tests. (Discussion) *Educational and Psychological Measurement,* 1962, **22,** 35–39.

Flanagan, J. C., Dailey, J. T., Shaycoft, M. F., Gorham, W. A., Orr, D. B., & Goldberg, I. *The talents of American youth: I. Design for a study of American youth.* Boston: Houghton Mifflin, 1962.

Gardner, E. F. Determination of units of measurement which are consistent with inter- and intra-grade differences in ability. Unpublished doctoral dissertation, Harvard University, Graduate School of Education, 1947.

Gardner, E. F. Value of norms based on a new type of scale unit. In *Proceedings of the 1948 Invitational Conference on Testing Problems.* Princeton, N.J.: Educational Testing Service, 1949. Pp. 67–74.

Gardner, E. F. Comments on selected scaling techniques with a description of a new type of scale. *Journal of Clinical Psychology,* 1950, **6,** 38–43.

Gardner, E. F. Normative standard scores. Symposium: Standard scores for aptitude and achievement tests. *Educational and Psychological Measurement,* 1962, **22,** 7–14.

Gardner, E. F. The importance of reference groups in scaling procedure. In A. Anastasi (Ed.), *Testing problems in perspective.* Washington: American Council on Education, 1966. Pp. 272–280.

Gulliksen, H. *Theory of mental tests.* New York: Wiley, 1950.

Guttman, L. The basis for scalogram analysis. In S. A. Stouffer et al., *Studies in social psychology in World War II.* Vol. IV. *Measurement and prediction.* Princeton, N.J.: Princeton University Press, 1950. Pp. 60–90.

Harris, C. W. (Ed.) *Problems in measuring change.* Madison: University of Wisconsin Press, 1963.

Hull, C. L. The conversion of test scores into series which shall have any assigned mean and degree of dispersion. *Journal of Applied Psychology,* 1922, **6,** 298–300.

Keats, J. A. A statistical theory of objective test scores. Hawthorn, Victoria: Australian Council for Educational Research, October 1951.

Keats, J. A., & Lord, F. M. A theoretical distribution for mental test scores. *Psychometrika,* 1962, **27,** 59–72.

Kelley, T. L. Ridge-route norms. *Harvard Educational Review,* 1940, **10,** 309–314.

Kelley, T. L. *Fundamentals of statistics.* Cambridge, Mass.: Harvard University Press, 1947.

Kish, L. *Survey sampling.* New York: Wiley, 1965.

Lawley, D. N. On problems connected with item selection and test construction. *Proceedings of the Royal Society of Edinburgh,* 1942–43, 61 (Section A, Part III), 273–287.

Lazarsfeld, P. F. Chaps. 10 & 11. In S. A. Stouffer et al., *Studies in social psychology in World War II.* Vol. IV. *Measurement and prediction.* Princeton, N.J.: Princeton University Press, 1950.

Lennon, R. T. Equating nonparallel tests. *Journal of Educational Measurement,* 1964, **1,** 15–18.

Lennon, R. T. Norms: 1963. In A. Anastasi (Ed.), *Testing problems in perspective.* Washington: American Council on Education, 1966. Pp. 243–250.

Levine, R. S. Equating the score scales of alternate forms administered to samples of different ability. Educational Testing Service *Research Bulletin,* 1955, No. 23.

Levine, R. S. Estimated national norms for the Scholastic Aptitude Test. Educational Testing Service *Statistical Report,* 1958, No. 1.

Lindquist, E. F. Factors determining reliability of test norms. *Journal of Educational Psychology,* 1930, **21,** 512–520.

Lindquist, E. F. Sampling in educational research. *Journal of Educational Psychology,* 1940, **31,** 561–574.

Lindquist, E. F. Selecting appropriate score scales for tests. (Discussion) In *Proceedings of the 1952 Invitational Conference on Testing Problems.* Princeton, N.J.: Educational Testing Service, 1953. Pp. 34–40.

Lindquist, E. F. Norms by schools. In A. Anastasi (Ed.), *Testing problems in perspective.* Washington: American Council on Education, 1966. Pp. 269–271.

Lindquist, E. F., & Hieronymus, A. N. *Iowa Tests of Basic Skills: Manual for administrators, supervisors, and counselors.* New York: Houghton Mifflin, 1964.

Lord, F. M. Notes on comparable scales for test scores. Educational Testing Service *Research Bulletin,* 1950, No. 48.

Lord, F. M. A theory of test scores. *Psychometric Monographs,* 1952, No. 7. (a)

Lord, F. M. The scale proposed for the Academic Ability Test. Educational Testing Service *Research Memorandum,* 1952, No. 3. (b)

Lord, F. M. On the statistical treatment of football numbers. *American Psychologist,* 1953, **8,** 750–751.

Lord, F. M. Equating test scores—a maximum likelihood solution. *Psychometrika,* 1955, **20,** 193–200. (a)

Lord, F. M. The standard error of norms and the standard error of measurement. Educational Testing Service *Research Memorandum,* 1955, No. 16. (b)

Lord, F. M. A survey of observed test-score distributions with respect to skewness and kurtosis. *Educational and Psychological Measurement,* 1955, **15,** 383–389. (c)

Lord, F. M. The measurement of growth. *Educational and Psychological Measurement,* 1956, **16,** 421–437.

Lord, F. M. Do tests of the same length have the same standard errors of measurement? *Educational and Psychological Measurement,* 1957, **17,** 510–521.

Lord, F. M. Further problems in the measurement of growth. *Educational and Psychological Measurement,* 1958, **18,** 437–451.

Lord, F. M. Test norms and sampling theory. *Journal of Experimental Education,* 1959, **27,** 247–263.

Lord, F. M. Large-sample covariance analysis when the control variable is fallible. *Journal of the American Statistical Association,* 1960, **55,** 307–321.

Lord, F. M. Estimating norms by item-sampling. *Educational and Psychological Measurement,* 1962, **22,** 259–267.

Lord, F. M. Elementary models for measuring change. In C. W. Harris (Ed.), *Problems in measuring change.* Madison: University of Wisconsin Press, 1963. Pp. 21–38.

Lord, F. M., & Novick, M. R. *Statistical theories of mental test scores.* Reading, Mass.: Addison-Wesley Publishing Co., 1968. Chaps. 17–20.

Lorge, I., Thorndike, R. L., & Hagen, E. *Technical manual for the Lorge-Thorndike Intelligence Tests, Multi-Level Edition.* Boston: Houghton Mifflin, 1966.

McCall, W. A. *Measurement.* New York: Macmillan, 1939.

McGee, V. E. Towards a maximally efficient system of braiding for Scholastic Aptitude Test equating. In S. S. Wilks (Ed.), *Scaling and equating College Board tests.* Princeton, N.J.: Educational Testing Service, 1961. Pp. 86–96.

McNemar, Q. *The revision of the Stanford-Binet scale.* New York: Houghton Mifflin, 1942.

McNemar, Q. On growth measurement. *Educational and Psychological Measurement,* 1958, **18,** 47–55.

Manning, W. H., & DuBois, P. H. Correlational methods in research on human learning. *Perceptual and Motor Skills,* 1962, **15,** 287–321.

Mollenkopf, W. G. A study of secondary school characteristics as related to test scores. Educational Testing Service *Research Bulletin,* 1956, No. 6.

Pearson, K. On the relationship of intelligence to size and shape of head, and to other physical and mental characters. *Biometrika,* 1906, **5,** 105–146.

Rasch, G. *Probabilistic models for some intelligence and educational tests.* Copenhagen, Denmark: The Danish Institute for Educational Research, 1960.

Schrader, W. B. Norms. In C. W. Harris (Ed.), *Encyclopedia of educational research.* (3rd ed.) New York: Macmillan, 1960. Pp. 922–927.

Schultz, M. K., & Angoff, W. H. The development of new scales for the Aptitude and Advanced Tests of the Graduate Record Examinations. *Journal of Educational Psychology,* 1956, **47,** 285–294.

Science Research Associates. Iowa Tests of Educational Development: Technical report (unpublished manuscript). Chicago: Science Research Associates, 1966.

Seashore, H., Wesman, A., & Doppelt, J. The standardization of the Wechsler Intelligence Scale for Children. *Journal of Consulting Psychology,* 1950, **14,** 99–110.

Stevens, S. S. Mathematics, measurements, and psychophysics. In S. S. Stevens (Ed.), *Handbook of experimental psychology.* New York: Wiley, 1951. Pp. 1–49.

Swineford, F., & Fan, C.-t. A method of score conversion through item statistics. *Psychometrika,* 1957, **22,** 185–188.

Terman, L. M., & Merrill, M. A. *Measuring intelligence.* New York: Houghton Mifflin, 1937.

Terman, L. M., & Merrill, M. A. *Stanford-Binet Intelligence Scale.* New York: Houghton Mifflin, 1960.

Thorndike, E. L., Bregman, E. O., Cobb, M. V., & Woodyard, E. *The measurement of intelligence.* New York: Columbia University, Teachers College, Bureau of Publications, 1927.

Thorndike, R. L. Community variables as predictors of intelligence and academic achievement. *Journal of Educational Psychology,* 1951, **42,** 321–338.

Thorndike, R. L. *The concepts of over- and under-achievement.* New York: Columbia University, Teachers College, Bureau of Publications, 1963.

Thorndike, R. L. Intellectual status and intellectual growth. *Journal of Educational Psychology,* 1966, **57,** 121–127.

Thurstone, L. L. A method of scaling psychological and educational tests. *Journal of Educational Psychology,* 1925, **16,** 433–451.

Thurstone, L. L. The mental age concept. *Psychological Review,* 1926, **33,** 268–278.

Thurstone, L. L. A law of comparative judgment. *Psychological Review,* 1927, **34,** 273–286.

Thurstone, L. L. The absolute zero in intelligence measurement. *Psychological Review,* 1928, **35,** 175–197. (a)

Thurstone, L. L. Attitudes can be measured. *American Journal of Sociology,* 1928, **33,** 529–554. (b)

Thurstone, L. L. Primary mental abilities. *Psychometric Monographs,* 1938, No. 1.

Thurstone, L. L. The calibration of test items. *American Psychologist,* 1947, **2,** 103–104.

Thurstone, L. L., & Chave, E. J. *The measurement of attitude.* Chicago: University of Chicago, 1929.

Toops, H. A. A proposal for a standard million in compiling norms. *Ohio College Association Bulletin,* No. 125. (c. 1939).

Torgeson, W. S. *Theory and methods of scaling,* New York: Wiley, 1958.

Tucker, L. R. Academic Ability Test. Educational Testing Service *Research Memorandum,* 1951, No. 17.

Tucker, L. R. Scales minimizing the importance of reference groups. In *Proceedings of the 1952 Invitational Conference on Testing Problems.* Princeton, N.J.: Educational Testing Service, 1953. Pp. 22–28.

Tucker, L. R, Damarin, F., Messick, S. A base-free measure of change. *Psychometrika,* 1966, **31,** 457–473.

Votaw, D. F., Jr. Testing compound symmetry in a normal multivariate distribution. *Annals of Mathematical Statistics,* 1948, **19,** 447–473.

Wilks, S. S. Sample criteria for testing equality of means, equality of variances, and equality of covariances in a normal and multivariate distribution. *Annals of Mathematical Statistics,* 1946, **17,** 257–281.

Wilks, S. S. (Ed.) *Scaling and equating College Board Tests.* Princeton, N.J.: Educational Testing Service, 1961.

Wright, B. D. Sample-free test calibration and person measurement. In *Proceedings of the 1967 Invitational Conference on Testing Problems.* Princeton, N.J.: Educational Testing Service, 1968. Pp. 85–101.